SUPPLEMENT TO
THE SYMPHONIES OF
JOSEPH HAYDN

By the same author

The Symphonies of Joseph Haydn
The Collected Correspondence and London Notebooks of Joseph Haydn
The Mozart Companion
Music in Eighteenth Century Austria (*in preparation*)

SUPPLEMENT TO
THE SYMPHONIES OF
JOSEPH HAYDN

BY
H. C. ROBBINS LANDON

LONDON
BARRIE AND ROCKLIFF

CONTENTS

ILLUSTRATIONS

FOREWORD

Those readers who own my book, *The Symphonies of Joseph Haydn*, may find these *corrigenda* and *addenda* useful. The first two sections were originally published in the *Music Review*, Vol. 19 No. 4 (November 1958, pp. 311–319) and Vol. 20 No. 1 (February 1959, pp. 56–70), and I am much indebted to *Music Review's* editor, Mr. Geoffrey Sharp, for his kindness in allowing us to reprint them here, with slight alterations which bring them still more up to date.

It is chastening for an author of a scholarly work (especially if the subject, as in Haydn's case, has yet some further secrets to reveal) to see how quickly the details of his research require supplementing. While the basic facts and the general observations will, it is hoped, remain valid, at least for a generation (by which time a new viewpoint is often needed), one must expect the scientific accuracy of such a book to need a periodic re-examination in the light of new discoveries. Those who know *The Symphonies* will see, from the present supplement, how many important manuscript sources in Hungary and Czechoslovakia remained to be examined critically.

Gradually, however, we are gathering together all the known manuscripts and early copies that must inevitably constitute our knowledge of Haydn's music. In the Autumn of 1960, the author was able to examine the Roumanian libraries and archives; the great hopes we had all placed on Grosswardein (Oradea Mare), where Michael Haydn and Dittersdorf were *Kapellmeister*, proved to be unfounded, for in the turbulent events at the end of the Second World War, the famous archives in the Archbishop's *Residenz* were either destroyed or dispersed. There now remains Russia, from whose State Archives I was fortunate enough to receive valuable Haydn autographs, the existence of which was not known even to scholars (*e.g.* the 'Overture' in D, Hoboken Ia:4, which Haydn marks 'Finale', thus raising a number of new problems). I think we may safely assume that when Russia's treasures are known to the Western world, the collecting of Haydn sources will be substantially completed. This is, of course, just the beginning. With so much of Haydn's music unpublished, and now that the German Joseph Haydn Institut (who are slowly publishing the Collected Edition) has lost Professor Jens Peter Larsen, thus leaving the edition without any known Haydn scholars at all, there seemed only one course to follow: for me to issue, as quickly as possible, this vast *corpus* of unpublished Haydn,

some of which has come down to us in one single source in an obscure
Eastern European library. To this end, I have secured the co-operation of
two Viennese publishers, the Universal Edition and Verlag Doblinger, and
between these two enterprising houses, some two hundred unpublished or
unavailable works by Haydn—including operas, orchestral music, vocal
music and chamber music from the earliest period to the London visits—
will be available in critical editions by the end of 1961. By that time, there
will no longer be any excuse to talk of 'The unknown Haydn': and by that
time, even my own research will have succeeded in putting *The Symphonies
of Joseph Haydn* still more out of date—a fact which would be more melan-
choly were it not for the joy of having so much glorious music available to
every musician and music-lover.

Meanwhile, my Hungarian colleagues have been meticulously sifting the
material of the vast Esterházy Archives in Budapest; and having been
allowed, on four recent trips to Hungary, to examine personally a large part
of this material, it is safe to say that our knowledge of the Esterházy years,
and thus of the greater part of Haydn's artistic life, has been revolutionized.
The Hungarians are currently engaged in publishing this gigantic mass of
material[1] in the original German, and when all of it has appeared, we shall be
able, for the first time, to form a balanced judgement of Haydn's life and works.

In a sense, then, my book on the symphonies has turned out to be an
'interim study', interim in that it deals with but a part of Haydn's music
and interim, too, in that so many new documents of his life have come to
light in the Esterházy Archives. Perhaps the most important of these are
available in the *Collected Editions of Haydn's Letters*; but there are many
more yellowing pages in the Esterházy Archives that tell us much of Haydn's
day-to-day life, his duties as *Kapellmeister*, his dealings with fellow musicians
and court officials; and it is inevitable that the sum total of these sources
will show Haydn, the man (and thus Haydn the musician, too) in a different,
and in any case far more complete, light than has ever been the case since
his death in 1809.

This modest attempt at a supplement, therefore, may be said to round
off, as best it can for the time being, a book, the lack of finality of which
no one realises more clearly than the author.   H. C. R. L.
Buggiano Castello,
January, 1961.

---

[1] One result, the most interesting book, *The Fairyland of Esterháza* by Mátyás Horányi,
is about to be published by Barrie & Rockliff.

ACKNOWLEDGMENT

© The Czech section of this book was kindly read and corrected by Dr. Jan Matějček, Prague; author and publisher wish to express their thanks to him.

I. THE CZECH SOURCES

Since the publication of the two sections of 'Errata and Corrigenda' in *Music Review*, the author has at last been able to go to Czechoslovakia, and to make the long-needed examination of the Haydn sources there. It was obvious, even after examining the enormous material at Prague, that apart from the Austrian and South German collections, the Haydn manuscript material in Czechoslovakia is among the most important, historically and textually, that is still extant. It is almost incredible that no one hitherto has examined it in detail. The reasons for this are many and varied, but perhaps the most important is that the manuscripts now in the National Museum in Prague came from aristocratic and ecclesiastical, *i. e.* private, libraries all over the country. As the author has had occasion to notice, the previous owners of these libraries (we refer in particular to the aristocracy now living abroad) usually had no idea of the value of their music library, and in some cases no idea that they had even *had* a music library. Thus, these precious Haydn manuscripts spread throughout Czechoslovakia were practically inaccessible, because scarcely anyone knew even of their existence. There is absolutely no excuse, however, that these sources — which have been in Prague for many years now — are missing in Hoboken. Leaving aside the symphonies, our examination of the Czech collections revealed several lost works: at least one march and three divertimenti, indubitably genuine, which are entirely missing in Hoboken (that is, not only the sources, but the works themselves). We do not hesitate to state that the lack of the Czech sources in Hoboken has rendered that catalogue of even less value — as far as the manuscript sources in it are concerned — than was hitherto the case.[1]

The following lists of material have been divided into two basic sections: (I) the manuscripts of Haydn's symphonies, listed under the name of the library, including a short note on the library and the other (non-symphonic) works found in it; (II) a list of the new sources found in Czechoslovakia which affect the spurious Haydn symphonies; as will be seen, this list

---

[1] A very severe but, in our opinion, entirely just criticism of Hoboken's work appeared in *Music Review*, Vol. XVIII, No. 4 (November 1957), pp. 330 *ff*. Unfortunately — and this is said without arrogance — most of the other reviewers were too unfamiliar with the material to be able to judge the catalogue's accuracy.

includes several new attributions of spurious works, the authors of which were not hitherto known, and some 'new' doubtful works. Unfortunately the scope of the present book does not permit us to include the list of non-symphonic spurious Haydn works, the correct authors of which we were able to locate in various Czech libraries; the author hopes, however, to present this new evidence at another time.

The material in the former archives of Count Pachta was included in Hoboken, and is therefore not given here. The names of the various libraries are listed first in Czech, followed by the old German name — if different — in brackets.

Osek (*now National Museum, Prague*)

The Haydn manuscripts of this great monastery are among the earliest we have; in some cases they antedate all other known manuscripts, even those of Göttweig Abbey in Austria. Apparently the monks at Osek procured their music partly from Prague, but partly from Vienna, too, which would explain the early date of many of the Haydn symphonies. Apart from symphonies, Osek owns chamber music and the only known copy of 'XII Menuette' (later enlarged to fourteen pieces) for orchestra by 'Giuseppe Haydn'; these would appear to be genuine, hitherto lost minuets of the period *c.* 1760–1770. Most of the earlier symphonies were procured by a Pater Leopold, some others by P. Leonard Dohnt.

Symphony	Cat. No.	Remarks (*if any*)
3	2946A	
4	486A	
9	2697A	Erroneously listed under Gassmann (!)
13	290A	Erroneously listed under 'Wanhall' (*i. e.* Vaňhal) (!)
14	555A	'Pro / Monasterio Ossecensi'
15		The first movement is used as 'Sinfonia' to an anonymous Cantata, and is scored for 2 oboes, 2 clarini and strings
17	2680A	Scored for 2 oboes, 2 horns, strings (see corrected instrumentation in Appendix I of my book)
23	893A	'F: Leopoldi Oss: Pl: 1769'
24	2683A	

Symphony	Cat. No.	Remarks (if any)
26	2681A	'P. Leopoldi Oss. prof. / 1770', the earliest known copy of the work, antedating those at Göttweig and Herzogenburg (hitherto the earliest known *MSS.*) by two years
28	2682A	'P. Leopoldi Oss. prof. / 1770'
29	186A	'P. Leopoldi Oss. rofm [?] 1770'
36	188A	
41	896A	'P. Leopoldi Osseci professi Anno 1771' — together with Göttweig, the earliest dated source. Here scored with the trumpets and drums
43	552A	'Procuravit pro / Monasterio R: P: / Leonardus Dohnt / loci professus'
44	887A	'Procuravit pro Monasterio Ossecensi R: P: Leonardus Dohnt Professus'
45	2672A	The finale only, transposed into E minor (a late copy)
47	2668A	'Describi fecit pro / Monasterio Ossecensi / P. Eustachius Fischer / Loci professus'
48	187A	'P. Leonardi O.C. P. C.', the *MS.* with 'Corni 2 in C alto' but no trumpets and timpani
49	189A	'P. Leopoldi Oss. rof. [?] 1771'
51	332A	
52	2678A	'Ex Rebus / Antony Cron'
53	192A	'Procurata á P. Leonardo Dont p. t. Reg. chori'. No introduction to the first movt., scoring for fl., 2 ob., 2 fag., 2 cor., 2 trpt., timp., str.; with Finale of Version B
54	189A	'Pro monasterio Ossecensi'. No introduction, no trumpets & timp.
57	333A	No timpani
60	336A	Title page lists trumpet parts which are, however, missing
64	337A	
65	891A	'Procuravit pro Monasterio R: P: Leonardus Dohnt loci professus'
66	191A	'Procurata á P. Leonardo Dont [*sic*] p. t. Reg. chori'
67	335A	[remark as above, for No. 66]
69	183A	[ditto]
76	338A	'Fine / Die 7 October 1799' (at end of Basso part)
79	2677A	'P. Legior [?]'
82	131A	No trumpet parts

Symphony	Cat. No.	Remarks (*if any*)
89	2669A	'A. W. 1814' in a later hand
93	2673A	
94	190A	
97	2670A	
103	334A	'A[.] Wolff. 1800'
104	401A	

Kačina (now National Museum, Prague)

Kačina was the castle of the Counts Chotek, and here we encounter the first authentic manuscripts in the Prague library. There are in fact so many — relatively speaking — and from such different periods, ranging from Joseph Elssler's copy of Symphony No. 41 to the Johann Elssler copies of *The Storm* (in German) and the London Symphonies, that one is tempted to think that Haydn must have had some kind of personal connection with the Chotek family. Apart from *The Storm*, Johann Elssler also copied parts to the overtures of *Armida* and *La Vera Costanza*. There are two symphonies, one of which was originally anonymous and one of which lost its title page; someone added Haydn's name on both of these works — one is in F Major, the other in G — but they cannot even be considered 'doubtful' Haydn and have not been included here. Jan LaRue kindly informs me that both works are in fact by Schwindl; that in F major is Op 2, No. 5, and that in G Op. 2, No. 2; Op. 2 was issued by Hummel in 1768 and reprinted *inter alia* by C. & S. Thompson (copy in British Museum, R. M. 16. f. 16) in London.

Happily, a number of thematic catalogues of the Chotek library has been preserved. The earliest of these is simply entitled 'Catalogo' and includes Haydn chamber music and two symphonies, Nos. 27 (the parts of which are no longer extant) and 41 (see below). Apart from this volume, there are 'Catalog / der / Harmonie / Stücke und / Türkischemusik', 'Catalog / der / Opern / Oratorien / und einzelnen / Singstücken' and 'Catalog / der / Kirchen / Musicalien'. The list of Haydn's symphonies still preserved is as follows:

Symphony	Old Cat. No.	Remarks (*if any*)
41		An authentic copy by Joseph Elssler written on Esterházy paper with the characteristic jumping stag (of the period after *c.* 1770) and the letters

Symphony	Old Cat. No.	Remarks (*if any*)
		'IGW'. The interesting thing about the source is that it lacks — also on the title page — the trumpet and timpani parts (which are indubitably genuine and are preserved *inter alia* in the copy of the work in the Esterházy Archives at Budapest). Their lack here suggests that they may have been added later, as Haydn so often did. The horn parts are marked 'Corno Primo in Hoch C', *etc.*
45	Kl. II, A3, No. 55	Called 'Urlaubs- / Sinfonia in Fis'
55	Kl. II, A3, No. 65	'Joh: Jos: Rabe.'
60	Kl. II, A3, No. 72	
63		Second movement under anonymous for pianoforte solo, 'La Roxelane'
81	Kl. II, A3, No. 70	
90	Kl. II, A3, No. 64	With the rare trumpet and drum parts
98	Kl. II, A3, No. 63	Fragments in the handwriting of Johann Elssler, together with André and Artaria parts of the London Symphonies. It would appear that the remaining Elssler parts were discarded when the prints were purchased

---

Frýdlant (*now National Museum, Prague*)

The music archives of Frýdlant (Schloss Friedland), the castle belonging to the Counts Clam Gallas, are among the most important in Czechoslovakia. It was here that the author located a hitherto unknown Haydn 'Marche Regimento De Marshall' for wind-band, a Haydn Cassatio for four horns and strings, one lost wind-band Divertimento (HV 3) and two undoubtedly genuine wind-band Divertimenti of which not even the *incipits* were known hitherto.[1] Apart from these lost or unknown works of which all except one are wanting in Hoboken, Clam Gallas own one of the two most important collections of the early wind-band music which Haydn must have written when in the service of Count Morzin (whose summer castle, it will

---

[1] These works have been edited by me and published in the series 'Diletto Musicale' of Verlag Doblinger, Vienna.

be remembered, was in Lukavec, near Pilsen, in Bohemia). The other
collection is at Kroměříž and will be dealt with in the course of this section.
The Clam Gallas sources, most of which were written on small oblong paper
of the size suitable for being attached to the wind instruments (as, indeed,
is the usual band practice today), are of the utmost significance and throw a
much needed beam of light into the obscurity of Haydn's Lukavec years.

The Clam Gallas library owns two important thematic catalogues of the
eighteenth century. The first one contains only arias and does not directly
concern us, but for the information of interested readers we herewith list
the title: 'Catalogo / Delle Carte di Musica / appartenenti alla / Sig /
Contessa Carolina Clam = / Gallas'. The second thematic catalogue, on the
other hand, is of the greatest interest, for it contains all the instrumental
music, including many Haydn symphonies. Its title is: 'Catalogo / Delle
Carte di Musica / appartenenti / al Sig Conte Cristiano / Clam e Gallas / da
me per conservare / Speer / Maest[ro] di Musica'. Here follows the list of the
Haydn symphonies; all the parts are still extant unless marked 'mancano'
or 'manca'; upon examining them, it was at once clear that they were
practically all made by Viennese professional copyists. Some of the original
titles are of considerable interest, for they are the earliest known sources to
contain the nicknames by which many of Haydn's symphonies are now
known (*cf.* Nos. 30, 48).

No. of Cat.	Symphony	Remarks (*if any*)
14	6	'Manca'
15	72	'Violino, flauto, Violoncello Conct. 2 oboe 4 corni oblig'

[Nos. 16–21 are crossed out in red crayon. In pencil is the note 'C[onte] Kinsky',
i. e. they were at one time borrowed by Count Kinsky; in fact they are no longer
missing]

16	40	
17	35	
18		Divertimento (called on the parts 'Sinfonia in G'), Hoboken II, G–1; this source bears a very close relation to that of Lambach Abbey in Austria; both may have been written by the same copyist. *Cf.* my (first) edition of the work, Verlag Doblinger, for a description of the Lambach *MS.*
19	29	
20	49	
21	58	
22	5	}'mancano'
23	13 (without timp.)	

No. of Cat.	Symphony	Remarks (*if any*)
24	39	
25	26	
26	41	With trumpets and drums
27	30	The title page of the parts reads 'Alleluja / Sinfonia in C ...'
28	31	
29	Divertimento in F, HV 20	
30	65	
31	42	
32	48	The title page of the parts reads: 'Santae Teresiae / In C / Sinfonia ...'. Readers will remember that this Symphony was supposed to have been composed for the Empress Maria Theresa when she visited Esterháza Castle in 1773. The Clam Gallas parts (from Vienna) originally had no trumpets and timpani, but parts for these instruments were added locally, possibly by *Musikmeister* Speer
33	44	
34	43	
35	45	
36	46	
37	52	
38	47	
39	57	

[Nos. 40–43 crossed out in red crayon and the word 'mancano' added]

40	60	
41	55	
42	54	Scoring: 2 ob., 2 fag., 2 cor., timp., *i. e.* the original form (see *Gesamtausgabe*, Series I, Vol. 5)
43	56	Scoring: with horns and drums, but without trumpets

[Nos. 43–55 added later, in another ink]

44	63	'Roxolane', no trumpets and drums
45	62	
46	74	
47	67	⎫
48	69	⎬ 'Mancano'
49	71	⎭
50	70	Scoring: no trumpets and drums (which, it will be remembered, Haydn added later)
51	75	Scoring: '2 corni ô clarini' and timpani

2

No. of Cat.	Symphony	Remarks (if any)
52	66	
53	68	
54	78	
55	76	

[The themes, but not the clefs and signatures, of the final entries are in still another ink and were obviously added still later than the foregoing ones]

56	77	

[The catalogue numbers now fall into utter confusion]

0	33	The parts include trumpets and drums, apart from the Frankfurt copy (see also *infra*, p. 54), the only extant *MS.* to contain them
5	28	
6	32	
6		Cassatio in D (the newly-discovered work, see *supra*)
7		The 'Toy' Symphony (see however *infra*, p. 27)
9	21	
10	38	
11	59	

As the observant reader will have noticed, the entries of this catalogue are quite patently *chronological*: naturally, many Haydn symphonies have been omitted, but those that are included follow a definite chronological pattern. For example, the entries 30–43 read something like the first pages of *Entwurf-Katalog* with the numbers mixed up; the symphonies run from c. 1771 (e. g. No. 42), to 1772 (Nos. 45, 46, 47 and many of the others which, however, cannot be dated so exactly), to 1774 (Nos. 57, 60, 55, 54, 56). The Count must have bought his new Haydn symphonies as quickly as they became generally available; perhaps he had a standing order with one or more of the Viennese professional copyists. It will also be obvious to students of Haydn that with Symphonies 76–78 (composed, as we now know, in 1782) the Count more or less stopped collecting Haydn; he would have purchased them about 1783 or 1784. Assuming — as I think the catalogue entries permit us to do — that the Count began collecting about 1768 or 1769, we have a fairly tight run of Haydn's symphonies for the next fifteen years. We hope that Czech scholars will uncover more information about the musical life in Frýdlant Castle and its connection with Haydn.

Doksy (*now National Museum, Prague*)

Schloss Hirschberg, owned by the famous Wallenstein family, whose name is so closely connected with Prague's history, was methodically set in order by some obscure German scholar just before the Germans occupied Czechoslovakia. His work is a prime example of the kind of German musicology which Anglo-Saxon scholars so abhor: working in a gigantic pile of slips of papers, systematic to the last dotted i and crossed t, the scholar never seems to have considered it advisable or necessary to inform the scholarly world of the great importance of the Hirschberg music collection. Unfortunately, its importance is not so much for Haydn as for the pre-classical symphony of *c.* 1750; but as I examined work after work by Haydn's precursors — almost all of them rare or completely forgotten — I realized that here, in the Wallenstein Collection, was one of the most vital links between baroque and classical. Here was the evidence that we so urgently need: what the Viennese and Italian symphonists — *i. e.* not the Mannheim school — were writing about 1750. It is devoutly to be hoped that these important archives will be examined and evaluated in detail. We could have had the evidence in 1938, if the busy German scholar had seen fit to describe that which he catalogued so assiduously.

The list of Haydn's symphonies follows:

Symphony	Remarks (*if any*)
3	
13	With the transposing timpani part (*i. e.* written in C–G) which someone added later in Haydn's autograph
24	
26	Listed under anonymous (Cat. 97A)
29	
32	With trumpets and drums
34	
35	

Town archives at Cheb (*Eger*)

A repository for various small collections in Western Czechoslovakia, Cheb has a number of fascinating sources, particularly Mozart *MSS.* which were not hitherto known; among them were copies of several piano concerti by

Johann Radnitzky whose name was in the early twentieth century more closely linked with Haydn than it should have been. The Mozart copies are partly signed 'Rky'. The fact that a relatively obscure town like Cheb should contain material of this kind shows what treasures we may expect when all of Bohemia, Moravia and Slovakia have been examined. The Haydn sources are rather late and appear to be, for the most part, local copies:

Symphony	Remarks (*if any*)
31	
45	'Al Uso di Cavaliere Giuseppe d'Adlersfeld da Egra gli 15[di] Mese Marzo 813'
48	With 'due Cornibus da Caccia in C alto' but originally without trumpet and drum parts which were, however, added later by another hand
51	
63	No trumpet and drum parts
65	
67	
69	
70	No trumpet and drum parts
75	With trumpets and drums in the first and last movts.

76, 77, 78, 79, 80,
94, 103, 104 (the latter patently a copy of a print)

Český Krumlov (*Krumau*)

Český Krumlov is dominated by the huge Schwarzenberg fortress, which includes, among many delightful objects, a beautiful baroque organ and an eighteenth-century theatre absolutely intact, complete with the old scenery, costumes, *etc.*, even to the musicians' candle-holders and ancient music stands. Here are the Schwarzenberg 'Central Archives', including the extensive music collection. Having known that Hoboken's Catalogue included Český Krumlov, we naïvely assumed that all the symphonies would be listed therein, and thus we examined only certain manuscripts which seemed of particular interest (*e. g.* the early and important copies of *Le Matin*, *Le Midi* and *Le Soir*). As it turned out, Hoboken's listing of the vitally important sources in the Schwarzenberg Archives is completely haphazard and inaccurate. The one really important source (a curious and obviously apocryphal wind-band Divertimento in F, Hoboken II, F–12) is listed in his catalogue as 'Kroměříž' — an item of information which caused considerable confusion when we tried to locate the *MS.* at Kroměříž. Altogether, Hoboken's almost *total* omission of the Haydn sources at Český Krumlov is a catastrophe. Most of the *MSS.* are of Viennese origin and textually of some importance. Since we are informed that Czech scholars are to publish a list of the Haydn sources there, we shall content ourselves with mentioning these *MS.* copies of Haydn symphonies listed as anonymous simply because the original covers (with the name of the composer) were torn off: Nos. 28 (II, 41f), 29 (II, 41k), 29 — another copy (II, 41m), 38 (II, 41i) and 59 (II, 41e). We hope that a complete list of the twenty-five odd Haydn symphony copies and other *MSS.* at Český Krumlov will be published in the near future; apart from Haydn, too, the collection is one of the most extensive in the country. The *MSS.* of wind-band music alone make it almost unique.

Brno

The National Janáček Music Library at Brno now houses a large number of collections from the province of Moravia. Some of these are so large that, as was the case in Prague, it was found more practical to list them separately. There follows here a list of the Brno material from various smaller libraries; wherever possible, the place of origin has been placed in brackets, after the present catalogue number. Needless to say, none of this material was included in Hoboken, though it has been available for many years now.

Symphony	Cat. No. and Place of Origin (where known)	Remarks (if any)
1	A324 (Lipník)	'Procuravit P. Fr. Georgius / profes. gradie p. t. Regenschori in annu II^{do} 1762, 10 Januarius.' 'Descripsit Joannes Schultz sintaxus stud. / Anno 1762.' The earliest dated source and the earliest *MS.* copy of a Haydn symphony (the Göttweig sources of 1762 are lost except for a single page of one work)
9	A21.155 (Dřevohostice Kůr)	

Symphony	Cat. No. and Place of Origin (where known)	Remarks (if any)
15	A141	
24	A322	
27	A24.201 (Kvasice)	Under anonymous, 'Del Sig: Inoto'. 'Pertinent Choro Guassicensi à 18 Martii 1772.' Scoring: 2 ob., str. (*i. e.* no horn pts.)
28	A6313 (Týn)	
34	A141	Wanting 1st movt. 'Ex partibus Wencesl. Seb. Benatek 1770'
35	A6653 (Rychnov)	
35	A21.464 (Brno Petrov)	
37	A24.220 (Kvasice)	'Ecclesiae Parochialis Guassicensis 1768' with pts. for 2 clarini and str.
42	A21.748 (Brno Petrov)	Incomplete
56	A14.563 (Olomouc)	Scoring incl. '2 Corni e Clarini'
60	A14.562 (Olomouc)	
69	A21.751 (Brno Petrov)	Anonymous (violin I wanting)
82	A309 (Lipník)	Incomplete

Náměšť Castle (Namest), *now at Brno*

Of great importance for its operatic tradition — several Haydn opera scores are included in the library, among them the second known complete copy of *Il mondo della luna* — Náměšť owns a considerable collection of Haydn symphonies, mostly of the middle period and not particularly early copies:

Symphony	Cat. No.	Remarks (if any)
4	A16.721	
7	A16.708	'Le Midi Concertant Sinfonia'
9	A16.717	'Zingarese . . .'
13	A16.726	With the timpani part
27	A16.730	Scoring: 2 ob., 2 cor., str.
32	A16.714	With the trpts. and timp.
35	A16.709	
41	A16.716	With the trpts. and timp.
48	A16.715	
53	A16.724	

Symphony	Cat. No.	Remarks (if any)
56	A16.735	The Guera print (see book, p. 701), here listed because of its extreme rarity
60	A16.713	With horns or trumpets
61	A16.722	With trpts. and timp.
67	A16.729	
69	A16.720	No trpts. and timp.
70	A16.725	
71	A16.711	
79	A16.728	
84	A16.727	
85	A16.710	
93	A16.723	
97	A16.719	

The Monastery of Nová Říše (Neureich), now at Brno

Symphonies 18 (A18.265, the first two movts. arr. as 'Duetto ex G', 'Ex Rebus Balthasar Seb. Berger mpria' for strings only), 42 (A17.731) and 65 (A17.733).

The Monastery of Rajhrad (Raigern), now at Brno

Symphony	Cat. No.	Remarks (if any)
24	A12.524	
24	A14.243	This second copy dated 1768
32	A12.493	With the trpts. and timp.
35	A12.530	Dated 1778
36	A12.526	Dated 1778
44	A12.495	
48	A14.244	No trpts. and timp.
52	A12.494	
56	A12.525	With both horn and trpt. pts.
66	A12.529	'1780 die 29 Aug'
69	A12.492	Dated 1783
75	A14.242	Dated 1789, with 2 clarini and timp.

The Collection at Kroměříž (Kremsier)

Somehow no one was quite prepared for the former castle of the *Fürstbischöfe* (Archbishops of princely rank) of Olomouc (Olmütz) at Kroměříž. We had all heard rumours of large Czech collections, uncatalogued and in general unknown to Western scholars; but none of us imagined to find a Haydn collection as important as Göttweig, or Melk, or Kremsmünster. Kroměříž, it may be flatly stated, is one of the most valuable Haydn archives extant, and for judging Haydn's early works (of the period 1755–1760) it is only rivalled by the sources in the former Berlin State Library. The two most important groups of works in Kroměříž are the early wind band music (some of which is found only here and in the Clam Gallas library — see *supra*) and in music for the keyboard. The staggering number of Haydn sources, and their early date, point to a direct connection with the composer — perhaps from the Lukavec period. The author hopes to make a through study of all the Haydn manuscripts at Kroměříž and to report on them at some future date.

The *Fürstbischöfe* were responsible for most of the precious collection in the castle; but a small, though interesting, part is formed by the manuscripts from the former *Piaristenkloster* (Monastery of the Piaristen order). In the following list, those *MSS*. from the Monastery are marked as such.

It is sad, under these circumstances, to have to report that most of the important Haydn sources in Kroměříž are missing in Hoboken — including *all* the music for wind-band, *all* the symphonies — the archives own half of all Haydn wrote — and almost all the most important concerto and other keyboard works. It is tragic that, because of this gross neglect of Kroměříž, not to speak of the other Czech collections, Hoboken is now completely out of date, scarcely three years after it was published.

Symphony	Cat. No.	Remarks (if any)
1	A-C	Piar. 'Des. Guido Kostler Poeta / 3 Septembris 1766'
1	IV, A111	
3	IV, A118	
5	IV, A120	
9	IV, A119	
13	IV, A115	No timp.
14	IV, A122	
18	IV, A113	Order of movts.: II–I–III–IV
21	IV, A117	

Symphony	Cat. No.	Remarks (*if any*)
22	IV, A127	2 fl. instead of cor. ingl.
23	IV, A112	
25	IV, A151	
28	IV, A127	
29	IV, A116	
34	IV, A114	Wanting the 1st movt.
35		From the castle at Olomouc (Olmütz)
38	IV, A130	With the trpts. and timp.
39		With 2 clarini instead of the B-flat horns; from the castle at Olomouc (Olmütz)
41	IV, A126	With the trpts. and timp. An arrangement for harpsichord as II, A51
42	IV, A161	
45	IV, A131	
48	IV, A138	
49	IV, A123	
49	A–C	Piar.
49	IV, A129	'Seminarii Cremsriensis / ad S. / Carolum Borromaeum 1773'
51	IV, A139	Scoring: 2 clarinets, 2 horns, 2 clarini (trpts.), str.
53	IV, A135	With the timpani, no trpt. pts.
54	IV, A140	No fl., trpt. or timp. pts.
55	IV, A132	With the (authentic) bassoon pt.
56	A–C	Piar. With pts. for horns or trumpets. Dated 1779
56	IV, A134	With pts. for horns *and* trumpets
57	IV, A137	With a part for flauto traverso
59	IV, A128	
62	IV, A141	
63	IV, A172	No trpts. and timp.
64	IV, A133	
66	IV, A149	
67	IV, A145	
68	IV, A147	
69	IV, A136	An arrangement for harpsichord (with the finale) as II, A49
70	IV, A144	No trpts. and timp.
71	IV, A150	
72	IV, A125	With pts. for 2 horns and 2 bassoons
73	IV, A143	

Symphony	Cat. No.	Remarks (if any)
75	IV, A152	With trpts. and timp.
76	IV, A153	
77	IV, A154	
78	A-C	Piar. Dated 1791
78	IV, A146	
79	IV, A155	An arrangement for harpsichord as II, A52
80	IV, A157	An arrangement for harpsichord as II, A78
81	IV, A156	Ditto as II, A50
84	IV, A159	
85	IV, A158	
88	IV, A160	
91	IV, A162	
93	IV, A163	

Symphony in B flat (HV 7), Appendix I 'B': *MS.* from castle at Olomouc (Olmütz)

Bratislava (Pressburg)

The centralization of the Slovakian musical manuscripts has not proceeded with the same efficiency as at Prague and Brno. When Professor Larsen and I examined the *MSS.* in the Academy of Arts and Sciences at Bratislava in the Autumn of 1959, we were able to find only a few copies of mostly secondary importance: Symphonies 9, 10, but also — to our surprise and delight — a beautiful copy on IAVG paper (watermarks: V, 1) by Joseph Elssler of Symphony No. 38, of which no authentic copy was hitherto known to have survived. The *MS.* was owned by the Serviten Monastery at Pest and is dated 1777. Most of the Serviten *MSS.* are now in the National Museum at Budapest (see *Haydns Werke in der Musiksammlung derNational-bibliothek Szechenyi in Budapest*, Budapest, 1959, pp. 98 *ff.*) and it is something of a mystery how the symphony manuscript got to Bratislava.

Budapest (National Museum)

An important series of manuscripts — not part of the Esterházy Collection — has been acquired by the library at Budapest. Included are many symphonies — also very early ones — from the library of a Lt.-Col. Fürnberg, who may have been a relation of the Count Fürnberg for whom Haydn wrote his earliest quartets. The copies are largely of Viennese origin, and some were written by a Viennese professional copyist to whom I gave the No. '2' in my book (see pp. 45 and 611). Readers are referred to the excellent catalogue of the Budapest collection, the title of which is quoted just above.

Czech sources for Appendix II

No. 1: Pichl also (a) Doksy Castle 66–A; (b) Osek Monastery 170; (c) Pachta Coll. XXII, E–21, as 'Pallas Dea' 'Fatta nel anno 1769'; (d) Prague Nat. Mus. XIII, F–137, 'Ex Rebus Antonii Borowy'; (e) Brno (Týn) A6329. In these sources, the tempo is 'Allegro con garbo'. Pachta has trpts. and timp. in the scoring (as at Kremsmünster).

No. 3: Koželuh also Clam Gallas Coll. Adalbert Gyrowetz in Prague Nat. Mus. XI, A101, from Domažlice.

No. 5: Mich. Haydn in Kačina (with C alto horns), 'Ad usum / Fidelis Candon [Landon?]', *cf. infra.* p. 51 (corr. to p. 706).

No. 6: Dittersdorf also in Osek Monastery 362–A, and in Brno (Lipník) A302.

No. 8: Vaňhal also in Frýdlant Castle 13–A and in Kroměříž IV, A335 (both in the *b* sequence).

No. 13: Ordoñez also (a) Osek Monastery 342–A and (b) Pachta Coll. XXII E–9.

No. 18: *Probable author: Koželuh (cf. 3)*: printed parts, Sieber, Paris (copy in the University Library, Prague, 59, A5757). This important source was discovered by Dr. M. Poštolka of the Prague Nat. Mus. Music Division.

No. 21: Leopold Hofmann also in Brno (Zám. Strážnice) A142.

No. 24: Dittersdorf also (a) Nová Říše (Brno) A18.256; (b) Brno (Zám. Strážnice) A138; (c) Brno (Lípnik) A316, dated 1771 'Ex Rebus Josephi Gelinek'.

No. 26: the curious 'Toy Symphony' now appears in several sources attributed like that at Melk, to Johann Michael Haydn; there are also a few early sources in Czechoslovakia under Joseph's name. In Kačina (Kl. II, A3, No. 54) the old *MS.* parts are listed as 'Berdoltsgadner Sinfonia . . . Del Sig^re Hayden'; in the Clam Gallas Catalogue, it appears twice, once under Joseph (see *supra*, p. 18) and once under *Cassationi* where it is listed as 'di Michel Hayden. Violino, Viola. Basso. Gugu. ratschen. orgelhen. Wachtel. Cimbelstern. Clarino in G. Corno in C. tamborini'. The Clam Gallas parts of this work are still extant. In the Schwarzenberg Archives at Český Krumlov, we find it, as Kl. II, 31 in *MS.* parts, with the title 'Sinfonia Per il [left blank] Violino Viola Kú Kú Ratshen Orgel Hühn [*sic*]

Wachtel Cimbl Stern Clarino in G Corno in C e Tamburo e Basso Del Sig. Mich:
Heyden' with an additional movement (between the Allegro and Menuet):

The last (4th) movement is marked 'Tre Volte Da Capo'. Thus we see that the
last word regarding the authorship of this work remains to be spoken; one thing,
however, seems ever more clear: that the *Sinfonia Berchtesgadolensis* is not under
any circumstances a composition of Joseph Haydn.

No. 29: Pleyel also (a) in Prague Nat. Mus. XV, A51, dated 1798, with the tempo
'Allegretto'; from Příbram; (b) Kroměříž, IV, A260.

No. 33: In Kvasice (Brno), the work's *MS*. parts are listed as 'Heyden' (Cat.
A24.219) 'Pertinet choro Guassicensi à 4. Aprilis 1772'.

No. 37: Vaňhal also in Frýdlant Castle 3–A, with pts. for 2 ob., 2 cor., 2 clarini,
timp. and str. and tempo as in Kremsmünster *MS*.

No. 40: Vaňhal also in (a) Frýdlant Castle 1–A; (b) Doksy Castle 106–A.

No. 43: Abel also in Clam Gallas Cat.

No. 48: Schmitt also in Clam Gallas Cat.

No. 49: Dittersdorf also in Pachta Coll., XXII, C7 and in Brno, A14.775.
Anonymous in Rajhrad Monastery (Brno) A13.265.

No. 50: Under probable author, add (2) Anton Filtz (*cf.* 85): *MS*. pts., Osek
Monastery 416–A, 'Sinfonia . . . Del Sig. Fils', 'F:P:J: / Oss. Prof.'.

No. 67: *Scoring:* 2 fl., 2 ob., 2 fag., 2 cor., 2 trpt., timp., str. Another important
and early *MS*. under Cibulka's name is at Kroměříž, IV, A25.

No. 69: *Scoring:* 2 ob., 2 cor., str. *Probable author: Franz Weigert: MS*. pts.,
Kroměříž, 'Sinfonia in D minor . . . Francesco Weigert', Cat. IV, A349; the work
has the customary four movts.

No. 73: Van Swieten ('Vansvitt') also in Doksy Castle.

No. 74: Vaňhal also (a) Frýdlant Castle 2–A; (b) Kroměříž, IV A332.

No. 75: Osek Monastery 2679–A, owns a copy of this work in parts with the second
movement (*Allegro con Spirito*) first, 'Del Sig. Hayden'.

No. 81: Pugnani also in Kačina Castle Cat. (under str. quartets).

No. 85: Under 'Bach' sources add (3) Clam Gallas Cat., Bach No. 19, for 2 ob.,
2 cor., str. See also corr. *supra*.

No. 86: Zimmermann also in Kroměříž IV, A367 as 'Echo Symphonia in Dis',
with a fl. pt.

No. 90: Dittersdorf also in Pachta Coll., XXII, B292.

No. 93: In Rajhrad Monastery as 'Hayden' A12.496.

No. 94: Van Swieten ('Wanswitten') also in Doksy Castle.

No. 100: Pleyel also in Osek Monastery 561–A, 'AW d[en] 31 July $\overline{790}$'.

No. 101: Wassmuth also (a) Osek Monastery, 'Musicalische Schlittenfahrt . . . Del Sig^{re} Wassmuth', 'pro Mario Osecensi'; (b) Clam Gallas Cat., Wasmuth No. 1, 'die Schlittenfarth [*sic*]'.

No. 104: Pleyel also in Osek Monastery, 734–A, '6 Nov 790', and in Kroměříž (IV A253) as 'Die Ankunft / Sinfonia in F'.

No. 106: Pichl also in Pachta Coll. XXII, E27, for 2 fl., 2 cor., str.

No. 109: Since publication of the first part of these *errata*, three new and important sources for this much discussed work have appeared, all under Gyrowetz's name: (a) Prague Nat. Mus., from Příbram, XI, A103, 'Del Sig. Girovetz'; (b) Kroměříž, IV, A101; (c) thematic cat., Raigern Monastery (*cf.* p. 23), No. 143 under symphonies.

No. 112: Vaňhal also (a) Doksy Castle 57–A ('Vanhall'); (b) Frýdlant Castle 31–A; (c) Kroměříž, IV, A342, dated 1769. Haydn in Piaristen-Kloster Kroměříž, Cat. A-C, 'Des[cripsit] Carol Stehna / absolutus Poeta 1774 Fine die 10 Septembris'.

No. 116: Filtz also in Prague Nat. Mus., XXII, C208 'Del Sig. Fils'.

No. 118: Hofmann ('Hoffmann') also in Doksy Castle (tempo: 'Adagio').

No. Hoboken I: A–5: this interesting symphony, published by Madame Berault together with five other works (three authentic, two spurious: see Hoboken under I: 11) in 1772 as 'Œuvre XIV' has thus far eluded positive identification. The enormous collection of Ditters symphonies in Osek Monastery reveals that the work is probably by him: *Probable author: Dittersdorf* (*cf.* 6): *MS.* pts., Osek, Cat. 414–A, 'F: Leopoldi / Oss. Prof. / 1769'.

No. 119: This Haydn-Ordoñez Symphony, which so baffled three experts, is found as Ordoñez in the Pachta Coll. (XXII, E5): a Viennese copy, scored for 2 ob., 2 cor., str.

No. 120: Vaňhal also (a) Osek Monastery 166–A, 'Fris Leopoldi O: P: 1769'; (b) Frýdlant Castle ('Del Sig. Wanhal') 28–A.

No. Hoboken I: A–8: the source is from the Piaristen-Kloster at Kroměříž and is signed 'Descripsit . . . 1770' (several copyists); Cat. A-C.

No. 124: Dittersdorf also (a) Brno (Lipník), A320, dated 1773 and copied by 'Josephi Gelinek' (see *supra*, No. 24); (b) Rajhrad Monastery (Brno), A12.230, 'Procuravit . . . 1768'.

No. 125: Schmitt also in Clam Gallas Cat.

No. 126: Schuster also in Kroměříž, IV, A308.

No. 129: Maldere also in Clam Gallas Cat.

No. 130: Dittersdorf also (a) Osek Monastery 746–A; (b) Rajhrad Monastery

(Brno), A12.231 'Ex Rebus Joannis Jos: Parliczek'.

No. 131: Vaňhal also (a) Prague Nat. Mus., XI, C21 'De musica Joan. Aug. Fibiger'; (b) Frýdlant Castle 176–A.

No. 133: Vaňhal also Frýdlant Castle 72–A.

The two above-mentioned doubtful symphonies not included in Hoboken or Landon are as follows: (1) Doksy Castle: 'Sinfonia / Con / Violini / Corni / Viola / e / Basso. / Del Sig:^{re} Giuseppe Haydn. / Coll[ationiert] H'[19] on oblong Italian paper with the watermarks: 3 half moons of decreasing size and the letter 'W' under an ornament; old cat. no. 'N^{ro} 51' on the top right-hand side of the title page. The second movement is in A, *Andantino*, 2/4 and the finale, *Presto*, in D, 3/8. The *incipit* of the 1st movt. is:

(2) Town Archives, Cheb (Eger). 'N° 110 / Sinfonia in C ... Del Sig: Hayden ...', scored for 2 ob., 2 cor., str. The *incipit* of the 1st movt. is:

II. *Andante*, F, 2/4; III. Minuetto & Trio, C and F, 3/4; IV. *Presto assai*, C, 4/4.

II. OTHER MATERIAL

ILLUSTRATIONS

Plate I (facing p. 16): penultimate line of caption should read 'phonies: Nos. 24, 38, 36'. Plate XVI: the original painting is now in the Pinakothek, Munich. Plates XXXIII and XXXIIIa: for 'Grace' read 'Crace'. Plate XXXIX: another original drawing, from Dance's own Collection, was sold at Sothebys on 23rd January 1957 and is now in the Vienna City Museum. The one reproduced in my book is now in the Royal College of Music, London. A third copy, used by Daniell for his engraving, is owned by Mr. Edward Croft-Murray, Richmond.

P. xvi: Under 'Germany', penultimate line, first name should read 'Dr. Johannes Maier'.

P. 3: Lines 1 *ff.* and n. 5: This Symphony (App. II, 109) has been hitherto found only under Haydn's name, though it is quite clear that Haydn did not write it. Its attribution to Gyrowetz, however, is now strengthened (one might go so far as to say assured) by a new source which Mr. Fritz Kaiser discovered in the Zentral-Archiv des deutschen Ritterordens, Vienna. This institution owns an interesting thematic catalogue from the theatre in Freudenthal (Austrian Silesia, now Poland), entitled 'Catalogue / des / Diverses Musiques'. As the first of five Gyrowetz Symphonies, we find the G major work in question; the *MS.* parts are also still extant, though incomplete. See also p. 29.

P. 10: Paragraph 3, line 2 should begin 'fonien / Del Sig: Giuseppe Haydn . . .'.

P. 12: N. 27, line 1, penultimate word should read 'Compositionen'.

P. 13: Line 10 should begin: 'Schmidt', another composer entirely! . . .'.

P. 14: Three lines from the bottom, read: 'is inscribed 'C[horo] Mellic. 1781'.

P. 18: List of operas: *Der Neue Krumme Teufel*, under References, delete 'Dies, Griesinger', substitute: R. Haas, 'Die Musik in der Wiener Stegreifkomödie' (*Studien zur Musikwissenschaft*, 1925). Libretto of this version in the Vienna Stadtbibliothek, 22200–A with the note: 'NB. Die Musique sowohl von der Opera comique, / als auch der Pantomime ist componiret / von / Herrn Joseph Heyden [*sic*]'. I suggest that *Der Krumme Teufel* is in fact identical with *Der Neue Krumme Teufel*. Incidentally, the work was performed at the Court Theatre in Donau-eschingen during the season of 1778–1779; but it was given by strolling players, who presumably brought their music with them, for despite an intensive search through the whole musical archives at Donaueschingen, I could find no trace of the performance material.

P. 18: *La Canterina* — first performance in 1767.

P. 18: *Lo Speziale* — instead of 'no overture' read 'II, 10' (EK).

P. 18: *Le Pescatrici* — first performance in 1770.

P. 18: *Philemon und Baucis*, Part I (Vorspiel) — first performance Esterháza, 2nd September 1773; Part II (actual *Singspiel*), ditto.

P. 18: For last opera in the list on p. 18, read 'Hexenschabbas'.

P. 19: *Armida* — first performance Esterháza 1784 (autograph completed 1783).

P. 26: Meanwhile, another copy of the A major Symphony under Ordoñez' name has been located, in the Fürstenberg Archives at Donaueschingen. The copy, in which there are no wind parts, is very early.

P. 28: Add to list of autographs at top of page: 92 PNat (rediscovered in 1956).

P. 34: Add Nos. 14, 49, 64; Frankfurt/M., Stadtbibliothek. These *MSS.*, with the Esterházy watermarks of a jumping stag and the letters 'IGW', are part of the long-lost 'Frankfurt-Sammlung' (see p. 48), which my colleague Ewald Lassen has recently discovered.

P. 35: Add Nos. 93, 94, 95, 96, 97, 98, 99, 101, 102, 103, 104 — *MS.* parts by Johann Elssler and another copyist (Joseph, Jr.?), corrected by Haydn. These parts, which except for the autographs are the most important sources for the Salomon Symphonies thus far discovered, will be discussed in more detail *infra*. Donaueschingen, Fürstlich Fürstenbergisches Hofarchiv.

P. 36: Franz Bernhard, Ritter von Kees (1720–1795) lies buried in the Parish churchyard at Brunn (Maria-Enzersdorf), near Mödling bei Wien.

P. 38: Add to bottom of last paragraph before list: Subsequently three more Symphonies (Nos. 6–8) from this collection were located in the Monastery of St. Peter, Salzburg: how they came to the Monastery is a complete mystery. No. 6= Sinfonia LXXX; No. 7=Sinfonia LXXXI; No. 8=Sinfonia LXXXII.

P. 41: First paragraph, five lines from bottom ('Glöggl's name appears only on one . . .') should read: 'Glöggl's name appears on three Symphonies (Nos. 52, 60 and 65), and he obviously owned No. 63 as well, though he did not sign it. Franz Xaver Glöggl (1764–1839), Johann's son, was in correspondence with Haydn'.

P. 48: N. 42 must be changed in view of the rediscovery of Symphony No. 92's autograph (1789), which is also dedicated to the Comte d'Ogny.

P. 49: Line 1: Krumau is Český Krumlov; Kromericz (line 2) is Kroměříž.

P. 52: Paragraph 2: The Sieber correspondence has now been recovered; it is printed in the *Collected Edition of Haydn's Letters and London Notebooks*, London (Barrie & Rockliff) 1959.

P. 52: Paragraph 4: The Monzani & Cimador edition of the London Symphonies is partly identical with that of André, partly with that of Simrock; Salomon may have supplied both André and Simrock with the music, or (and this is in my opinion more likely) he engraved the plates himself and gave Simrock and André

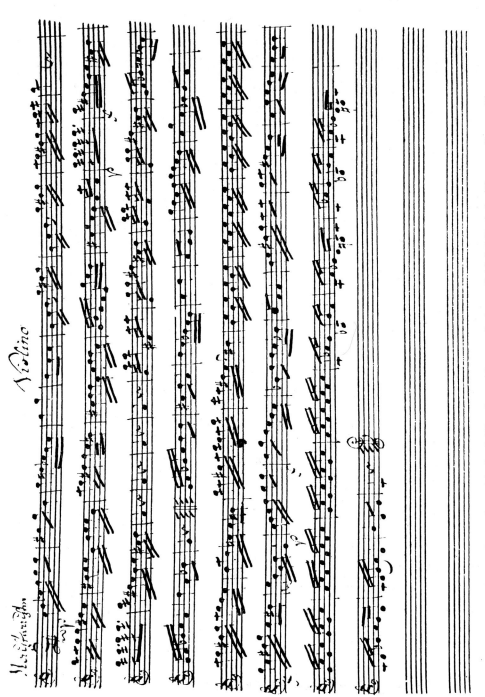

Folk-song, the melody of which Haydn used several times. Stiftsbibliothek, Metten. See p. 46.

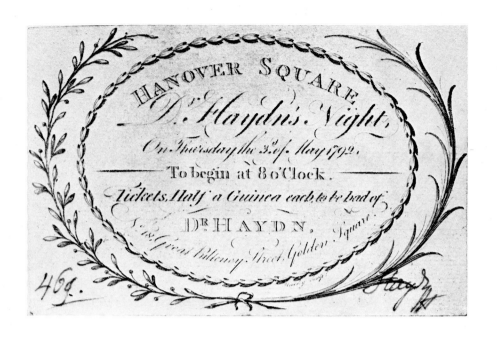

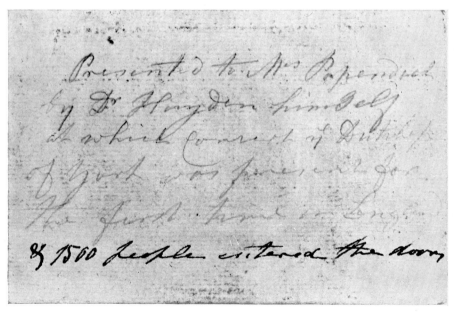

Ticket for Haydn's Benefit Concert in 1792 (Albi Rosenthal, London — Oxford).

the rights to use them. This theory would also explain why the German firms issued the works with plate numbers reading (in English) 'Haydn's Symphonys' and 'Salomon's Concert'. For all the available information concerning the various editions of the London Symphonies, see Hoboken's Catalogue.

P. 66: Paragraph 2, line 2 add to list of Symphonies No. 65.

Pp. 100 *ff.*: In the Winter of 1957, Christopher Raeburn and I made an extended visit to the Fürstenberg Library at Donaueschingen. This was one of the few major libraries in Central Europe which I had not visited personally when preparing material for *The Symphonies of Joseph Haydn*, and as it turned out, mine was a grave error of omission. Before proceeding to the sources there, I would like to express my gratitude to His Highness, Prince Fürstenberg, for his kindness and hospitality, not only in allowing us the complete freedom of his magnificent library and music archives, but also for inviting us to stay at the Castle.

I made a complete thematic catalogue of all the instrumental music in the archives, as a result of which a number of doubtful Haydn works could be attributed to the correct author. The doubtful Symphonies will be listed below, as they appear in my book. Apart from the actual sources, Donaueschingen owns a valuable thematic catalogue of 1803–1804, and several other, non-thematic catalogues which are of the utmost importance: thus we learn that the Court Theatre had performance material for the Haydn *Singspiel*, *Philemon und Baucis* (originally a marionette opera), which was finally destroyed in the early nineteenth century when it was no longer in use. Donaueschingen also contains perhaps the largest extant library of late eighteenth-century wind band music. It turns out that the Octet in F major for 2 oboes, 2 clarinets, 2 horns and 2 bassoons (Hoboken II, F–7) is actually a *Parthia* by Wranitzky (either Anton or Paul, both of whom were active in Vienna during Haydn's lifetime), Cat. Mus. Ms. 2062.

There are several operatic and oratorio arias by Haydn, some of which appear to be completely unknown: Mus. ms. 646 is the score of the aria from *Il ritorno di Tobia*, 'Come se a voi parlasse'; it is signed at the end 'artaria' (Haydn's publishing house) and is probably an authentic copy. Mus. ms. 669 is a Soprano Aria in B flat, 'Vada adagio, Signorina', in full score by Johann Elssler, the only copy in score of this insertion aria in Pietro Guglielmi's opera, *La Quakera spiritosa*, performed at Esterháza in 1787; Budapest has an autograph 'short score' in the material of the opera, but nothing else. Mus. ms. 667 is a *Recitativo e Rondo* 'Se ti perdo' (principal key: B flat) with solo viola and *cor anglais*. Charles Mackerras had found this work at Donaueschingen the year before, and subsequently played it on the Third Programme. The *MS.* parts were written by three copyists, one of whom is the so-called 'Kees Copyist' often referred to in my book; the source is Viennese in origin. But two factors suggest that — interesting though the piece is — Haydn is not the composer. The first is external: Haydn's name was added to the title page by the *Donaueschingen copyist*, and there is no trace of a composer

3

at all on any of the original parts. The source must have been sent to Donaueschingen as anonymous. Apart from its anonymity, moreover, I do not find the
work stylistically convincing. Mus. ms. 668 contains the parts of Haydn's Soprano
Aria, 'Caro, e vero', from the opera, *Armida*. Mus. ms. 646 is a Viennese copy of
'Come lasciar potrei', a 'Favorite Arias [*sic*] Del Sig^re Gius. Haydn 794 [1794]' in
piano score. Before proceeding to the principal find at Donaueschingen, I should
mention a series of Solfegii for soprano and *basso continuo*, Viennese manuscripts
which, though anonymous, would appear to be, both from outer as well as inner
evidence, lost works by Mozart. I hope to present this evidence, and to publish the
music itself, at another opportunity.

The principal find at Donaueschingen, however, was the discovery of eleven of
Haydn's twelve Salomon Symphonies in contemporary copies, almost entirely
written by Johann Elssler and thoroughly corrected and revised by Haydn himself. The only non-authentic copy is that of the 'Military' Symphony, which is
written by a local (?) copyist on 4° paper with the watermarks 'SCHIED'. Either
the original copy was played so frequently that it had to be replaced, or Haydn
did not supply the work (which is doubtful).

The other parts are written on several kinds of paper, partly Italian (*i. e.* copied
in Vienna) and partly on dated *English* paper (watermarks *inter alia*: ornate crown
with *fleur-de-lys* in coat-of-arms and G[eorge] R[ex]; *fleur-de-lys* over coat-of-arms
in form of a lyre with the letter 'W' and 'J WHATMAN / 1794'; and 'PORTAL
& BRIDGES' — *cf. The Symphonies*, p. 614). The curious thing is that both the
Italian and the British papers appear in the same Symphony. The first thought
that came to mind — namely, that Haydn sent the works from England —
therefore had to be discarded; for if that had been the case, naturally all the parts
would have been written on English paper. The second theory would be that
Haydn actually visited the Castle on his return to Vienna in the Summer of
1795: we know very little about Haydn's journeys to and from England, *i. e.*
exactly which routes he took. While I was examining the *MSS.*, Christopher
Raeburn kindly went through every number of the local Donaueschingen
Wochenblatt between July and December 1795: Haydn's visit would almost
certainly have been mentioned in the paper. Although Mr. Raeburn found no
mention of such a visit, he found another news item which, I believe, solves the
origin of the London Symphonies at Donaueschingen. The *Wochenblatt* of
2nd December 1795 includes the following:

Wien, den 19ten November.
Des Prinzen Karls von Fürstenberg Durchlaucht sind den 12ten dieses von Prag glücklich
hier angekommen, den 15ten und 16ten bey den Kaiserlichen Ministern, und Bottschaftern
von des Herrn Landgrafen Joachim von Fürstenberg Excellenz aufgeführt, und als dessen
künftiger Schwiegersohn vorgestellt worden.

Now the late London Symphonies were not yet known in Vienna, and on 18th

December Haydn arranged a 'grosse musikalische Akademie' in the Redoutensaal at which Beethoven played one of his own piano concertos (probably No. 2), and Haydn's Symphonies Nos. 102–104 were first performed in Vienna. It is not likely that Prince Karl heard the new works, and asked Haydn for copies of all twelve of the London Symphonies? Haydn, who probably guarded these works very carefully, had Elssler copy out some of the parts again; for the others he gave the Prince the actual parts he had brought back with him from London. It is therefore quite likely that these parts with the British watermarks were actually used in performances at the Hanover Square Rooms and King's Theatre under Haydn's personal direction.

A complete textual analysis of these new sources would require far more space than is at my disposal; when the Collected Edition of Haydn's music gets round to the London Symphonies, it is devoutly to be hoped that the editor will realize the unique significance of the Donaueschingen sources. A few points must suffice here. There was no room for the clarinet parts in the autographs of Symphonies Nos. 101 and 104; Haydn's own manuscript of No. 104's clarinet parts has survived; that of No. 101 has not, and it was not known whether the clarinets found in the early printed editions were genuine or whether they had been composed by one of André's or Hummel's hacks. The Donaueschingen copy of No. 101, however, includes the clarinet parts we knew from the early prints; and Haydn has given the parts his personal stamp of approval by adding a *fz* in Clarinet II towards the end of the Finale.

The additions which Haydn made consist of dynamic marks and phrasing (even *staccati*, of which Haydn added a great many in the flute parts of No. 103's Finale). Here is a typical instance which shows that the parts often include important details missing in the autograph. The return to the recapitulation in the first movement of Symphony No. 102 is marked by a long timpani roll. I have frequently been called upon to supervise recordings of the London Symphonies, and I have always told conductors to make a *crescendo* through bars 225 and 226 (Eulenberg, p. 18) even though this marking is wanting in Haydn's autograph. The Donaueschingen timpani part, in Elssler's large, flowing hand, contains a long swell under these very two bars.

The reader is asked to bear these copies in mind when using Chapter IV, pp. 100 *ff.* and Appendix I, Nos. 93–104, for reference.

P. 130: Line 2, 'anonymous volume': It turns out that the first part is a reprint of C. L. Junker's *Zwanzig Componisten*, Bern 1776; while the second part is a reprint of the same author's *Tonkunst*, Bern 1777.

P. 131: First paragraph, four lines from bottom, for 'composed almost exactly' read 'composed more than' (*cf. infra*).

P. 140: Three lines from bottom, read 'No. 60 (1774)': *cf. infra*.

P. 145: Ex. 26*a* and 26*b*: Last note of 2nd bar a″ (not g″).

P. 145: The three 'Quae metamorphosis' examples should read d' for the 4th note, not e'. Add the following sentence after the final example: 'The penultimate note g is omitted completely, and this rule applies to all other cases'. (Haydn thus explains in words that which he has shown in notes.)

P. 158: N. 55 should begin: 'See, for example, Symphony No. 44/III (*Adagio*), meas. 37; the harmony . . .'.

P. 159: First paragraph should end with following sentence: 'One exception is No. 84/I, where ↷ is used as follows: ♪♪ (meaning, of course, ♪♪ as in the little example in Haydn's letter, quoted below on the same page).

P. 159: N. 61: The letter is now owned by Mrs. Marguerite Manley, Scarsdale, New York, who kindly sent me a complete photostatic copy.

P. 164: Line 5: For the last three words read 'in such a manner'.

P. 165 (and *Errata*, p. 862): Delete *erratum*. One line is missing; between lines 3 and 4, add 'at Ex. [51*b*], and imagine at the same time the notes of the upper part'.

P. 166: First paragraph, line 6, for 'And in the least' read 'last'.

P. 172: N. 4, lines 2–3 'the Swedish Dictionary of Music' is *Sohlmans Musik Lexikon*, Stockholm 1950.

P. 175: Line 15: add '15' after No. '11.'

P. 189: Line 1: The Divertimento has also survived in Kroměříž; the library there kindly supplied a microfilm of the old parts.

P. 189: Ex. 7, Fag. bar 7: Add quaver rest between 1st and 2nd notes.

P. 190: Penultimate line: The Monastery of St. Peter, Salzburg, owns a set of anonymous *MS.* minuets (anonymous because the cover is no longer extant), scored for small orchestra; possibly they are by the local composer Anton Cajetan Adlgasser (1728–1777). In one of the trios, in G major, the composer uses the 'Lamentatio' melody in the second violin.

P. 214: No. 27, read 'Sondheimer, *Haydn*, London 1951'. At end of note, add: Dies undoubtedly took this idea from Gerber's 'Haydn' article in his *Historisch-Biographisches Lexikon der Tonkünstler*, Leipzig, 1790, p. 611, and Gerber in turn probably took it from the article on Haydn and other Austrian composers in the *Wiener Diarium* of 1766.

P. 218: Line 6, read '60(1774)': *cf. infra*.

P. 225: N. 35, line 2, after *Nepola* add '[Nespola?]'.

P. 242: Last line: Symphony No. 98 is also missing in HV.

P. 260: N. 22. At end of note, add: Symphony No. 28 also exists as a Baryton Trio: the *MS.* parts were formerly owned by Artaria & Co. in Vienna.

P. 262: Paragraph 3, first sentence: *Cf.* the St. Peter Minuets (*supra*, p. 190), wherein the melody is allotted to the second violin.

P. 265: First line after Ex. 23, read: '. . . Haydn wrote his *Capriccio* on the old folk-song . . .'.

P. 266: Last paragraph, line 4 should begin: *Sinfonia di caccia*; line 5 should begin 'in G and D, are expected . . .'.

P. 272: Line 5, read 'Prati' (not Proti), *i. e.* Alessio Prati; add correction to p. 857.

P. 273: Line 11 should read: '(. . . 1768); the *Stabat Mater* (*c.* 1767) . . .'. A hitherto unknown letter by Haydn to an official in the Esterházy administration throws entirely new light on the dating of the *Stabat Mater*. On 20th March 1768, Haydn writes: 'You will recall that last year I set to music with all my power the highly-esteemed hymn, called Stabat Mater . . .' (see A. Valkó, 'Haydn Magyarországi Müködése a Levéltári Akták Tükrében' (*Kodály Zoltán 75. születésnapjara* [Zenetudományi Tanulmányok VI], Budapest 1957, p. 651).

P. 273: Last line, third word, read 'Wyzewa'.

P. 276: Ex. 1 is in fact part of the Ballet Music in Gluck's *Paride ed Helena* (see my book, p. 315), and was again used in the French version of *Orfeo*. The other ballet is by Ordoñez (see below p. 60). It was Miss Rosemary Hughes who kindly pointed out the *Orfeo* quotation. In its original form, the Gluck ballet may be seen in Gluck's *Sämtliche Werke*, Abt. I, Bd. 4 (edited by the late Rudolph Gerber), Bärenreiter Verlag, Kassel, 1954, p. 64.

P. 286: N. 11, line 2, first word: read 'Eferding' (not Efferding).

P. 287: N. 12: Haydn's predecessor at the Esterházy Court, Gregorius Joseph Werner (1695–1766), wrote a series of *Lamentationes cum Sequentibus responsoriis* using the *Lamentatio* melody; *MS.* copies of the parts are preserved in the Sándor Wolf Museum at Eisenstadt. Haydn must have heard the works often.

P. 312: Concerning Haydn's *Stabat Mater*, see *supra* (note for p. 273).

P. 313: First paragraph, penultimate line, penultimate word; read 'beside'.

P. 313: Last two lines, read: 'It is typical that one of the arias in *La Canterina* should include two virtuoso . . .'.

P. 315: Paragraph 2, line 2, add full stop at end of line ('Cortine auf. Donnerwetter.' [Curtain up. Thunder]).

P. 339: First paragraph, penultimate line should read: '(or that part of the movement which . . .'.

P. 347: Ex. 2*a*: Remove the bracket '⌐—¬' in bars 8–9; add bracket under Vln. II, bars 5–8 |_____|.

P. 348: The last four lines should read: 'tension of the passage derives from the suspension in the accompaniment of the first subject's *b* section (marked *x* in Ex. 2*a*), which is now extended . . .' (*etc.*).

P. 349: Paragraphs 2 *ff.*: The Symphony was in fact composed in 1774, as was surmised from internal evidence. The following articles from the *Pressburger Zeitung*[1] of 6th July and 23rd November 1774, throw new light on the origins of the *Sinfonia per la Commedia intitolata il Distratto*:

Esterház, June 30.

In the Prince's absence, the Prince of Modena visited Esterháza, accompanied by an Italian gentleman. This evening there will be a German comedy, and *Der Triumph der Freundschaft* is the play which will be given. Tomorrow *L'infedeltà delusa*, Italian opera in 2 acts. The music is by Herr Joseph Hayden. This admirable composer has recently composed music for the *Lustspiel, Der Zerstreute*, which will be given by Herr Wahr's Company: connoisseurs consider this music to be a masterpiece. It is full of the musical humour, the good spirits and the intelligence which characterize Haydenesque productions. The connoisseurs are amazed on the one hand, whilst on the other the public is simply enchanted, for Hayden knows how to satisfy both parties; from the most affected pompousness he drops into doggerel, and thus Hayden and Regnard vie with each other in producing *distrait* caprice [*wer am launischesten zerstreut*]. The play's value is thus much increased. The music describes the content better and better as the play progresses, and as the actors become ever more *distrait*. It is also expected that this experienced composer will write music to Shakespeare's *Hamlet*. [6 July 1774.]

*   *   *

Tuesday, St. Cecilia's Day, *Der Zerstreute* was given. Herr von Hayden wrote a curious sort of music for it, which our readers will remember from earlier numbers of this paper. Suffice it to say here that it is admirable, most admirable, and that the Finale, upon incessant applause of the audience, had to be repeated. In this number, which is most effective, allusion is made to the distracted gentleman who, on his Wedding Day, forgets that he is a bridegroom and has to remind himself by tying a knot in his cravat. The musicians start the piece with great pomp, and it takes them some time to remember that their instruments are not tuned. [23 November 1774.]

P. 360: Paragraph 2: Delete everything from line 9 to end of paragraph ('any of the sources'). Substitute the following: The confusion in which the individual parts now stood progresses from source to source. The Esterházy *MS.* seems to be the earliest: it contains the new Minuet but also the original Finale. The flute and bassoon parts drop out after the third movement, and it is not clear whether the horns are to play *alto* or *basso*: they are marked *alto* in the Minuet, but they have no designation in the other movements.[18]

---

[1] Pressburg (Bratislava), where the coronation of the Hapsburgs took place, is just over the Austrian border in what is now Czechoslovakia. It was a centre of culture in Haydn's time; there was a good theatre, and many aristocratic families kept orchestras of their own, *e. g.* Prince Batthyáni, Count Erdödy, *etc.* Haydn was often in Pressburg to engage singers and visit friends. Opposite Pressburg is the beautiful Esterházy Castle of Kitsee (now Burgenland, Austria), where Haydn and the whole band occasionally entertained visiting nobility or royalty. The *Pressburger Zeitung* is a goldmine of information, and its significance is just now being realized.

P. 361 : Line 9, read 'rather than the composer's . . .'.

P. 361 : After Paragraph 1, insert the following paragraphs : The next development may be seen in an old *MS.* in the Monastery of St. Florian. This source includes the new finale but the flute part, like that in the Esterházy *MS.*, is marked 'tacet' after the Minuet. St. Florian's bassoon part, curiously entitled 'Violonzello e Fagotto', may derive from a new lost source even earlier than that in Budapest, for it would seem to be a cross between the original bassoon parts of the *Mondo* Overture and that of the Esterházy *MS.* The horns, too, are clearly marked *basso* in the first, second and fourth movements.

As we examine the other contemporary *MS.* sources, flute and bassoon parts for the Finale begin to appear : possibly Haydn added them himself at a later date. But there are discrepancies here, too : the bassoon part in the Melk source of 1781 (see p. 710) mostly doubles the bass or the 'cello part, whilst that of the other source in Melk plays only in the tuttis. In short Symphony No. 63 poses almost insoluble textual (and musical) problems.

P. 361 : Paragraph 2 line 3 : For 'It is probable' read 'It is possible'.

P. 378 : Fourth line from the bottom should read as follows : 'of high G and D, are not contained in the autograph (Public Library, New York City), but are found in old copies and are probably genuine'.

P. 380 : Paragraph 2, six lines from bottom, read : 'al Roviesco' (not Rovescio).

P. 388 : N. 48, last line : For 'and the three symphonies' read 'and the symphonies'. The German word (I have photographs of the autograph) is clearly *deren* (Genitive plural) and not *drey* : Haydn abbreviates the 'en' by a swish downwards. Thus he refers not to Nos. 76–78 but to the proofs of his *Sei Sinfonie* (Overtures). But positive proof of Nos. 76–78's date is provided by a little known Haydn letter to the French publisher Boyer of 15th July 1783, wherein he refers to the symphonies as having been written 'last year'.

P. 394 : N. 52 : The Aria was in fact written for a performance of Cimarosa's opera, *La Circe*, given at the Esterháza Theatre in 1789. Haydn also wrote other 'insertion' music for *La Circe* which is quite unknown.

P. 396 : Last paragraph of portion in smaller print : Readers are reminded that No. 92 was written expressly for the Comte d'Ogny in 1789.

P. 397 : Paragraph 2, lines 2–3 : The accompanied recitatives for baritone solo are by Frieberth, not by Haydn. For details the reader is referred to Hoboken's Catalogue.

P. 428 : Lines 4–5 should read : 'an open question : in the autograph proper they are now lacking (though Haydn may have put them on separate sheets which no longer exist), but the EH parts and the Oettingen-Wallerstein source include them. Curiously, the (very early) Sieber print at first issued the work without these instruments, but somewhat later engraved the timpani part and included it with the material, but without bothering to change the title page, where it is not listed. Charles Mackerras, who owns an important collection of Sieber prints, has two copies of No. 92, both with timpani: in one there is no plate number, and in the other the plate number was added, the title at the head of the page slightly altered, and one bar crossed out'.

P. 431: Paragraph 2, six lines from bottom read: 'from Notturno No. 3 in G' (not No. 5 in C).

P. 436: Paragraph 2 (square brackets): This catalogue was sold by auction in 'XXXVII. Autographen-Versteigerungs-Katalog', Leo Liepmannssohn, Berlin No. 91 (4th and 5th November 1907).

P. 442: Paragraph 6 should begin: 'SIGNOR DAVID and Signor[a] CAPPEL-LETTE . . .'.

P. 445: N. 3: Dr. A. van Hoboken, who has seen the autograph of this letter in a private collection in New York City, kindly informs me that it is dated '14mo di Marzo'.

P. 446: Middle of page: Charlotte Papendiek's husband, Christoph, was a flautist and had played in Vienna some years before (see Pohl II, 135): Haydn may have known him from Austria.

P. 461: Middle of page (large type): No. 92 was written in 1789. See *supra*.

P. 464: Eight lines from bottom, read: 'Mr. Brassy [*sic*] . . .'.

P. 467: Smaller print, paragraph 1, line 8: The Viennese-born Joseph Diettenhofer was still living in London in 1799 (see Gerber's *Lexikon, loc. cit.*, I, p. 891).

P. 471: Paragraph 2, line 1: A copy of the *Battle* Symphony, arranged for pianoforte trio by the composer and bearing his signature, is in BM, g. 161. c. (10).

P. 474: Penultimate line of *The Times* criticism: add comma after 'effect'.

P. 477: Line 1: The autograph (EH) is entitled *Madrigal*.

P. 484: Line 3: Read 'hereditary'.

P. 493: Eighth Concert. Johann Nepomuk Hummel (1778–1837), then not yet 14, was later (1804–1811) Prince Esterházy's Kapellmeister; Hummel was a pupil of Mozart's and later became a popular composer.

P. 495: Haydn's Benefit Concert: Albi Rosenthal, to whom I am much indebted for many kindnesses, owns two unique relics of the Haydn-Salomon Concerts: the only extant ticket, and the only extant hand-bill. The ticket is for this Benefit Concert and is engraved in blue ink; the text reads: 'HANOVER SQUARE / Dr. Haydn's Night / On Thursday the 3^{d}. of May 1792 / To begin at 8 o'clock. / Tickets Half a Guinea each to be had of / Dr. HAYDN, / No. 18 Great Pulteney Street, Golden Square'. All this is within a pretty ornamental border, and the card is signed 'Macky sculpt'. It measures 12×8 cm. The composer signed the card

'469 Haydn', and on the back, in pencil, is the following note: 'Presented to Mrs. Papendiek [see *supra*, p. 446] by Dr. Hayden himself at which concert ye Dutchess of York was present for the first time in England & 1500 people entered the door'. Mr. Rosenthal has long promised to write an article on these delightful finds. See also p. 546, *infra*.

P. 498: Lines 3–4 should read: 'it is in C major, and a score which the composer took with him to England and used there is now in possession of Mr. F. C. Adler (Saratoga, N.Y. and Vienna); recently . . .' *etc.* This is not one of the works in the King's Music Library.

P. 500: First paragraph in large type. Haydn seems to have been befriended by the Barthélemon family. Not only did he assist at this benefit concert, but he also gave a symphony at their concert in 1794 (see p. 526); and recently still more concrete proof of this friendship has come to light. The Stanford Memorial Library (Stanford University, California) owns both the original editions of Haydn's English Canzonettas. The first set is signed by Haydn (as was the whole of the first impression) and bears the following inscription: 'The Gift of the Author to Cecilia Maria Barthélemon', and on p. 9: 'I heard dear Dr. Haydn, sing this, with peculiar expression — with grateful recollection of his English friends.' The 'Second Sett' is inscribed: 'Cecilia Maria Henslow. I had the great pleasure to hear the famous Doct. Haydn play & sing his beautiful Canzonetts (in my youth) in my Dear Father's House at Vauxhall. Oh! what a treat it was! The dear good & respected Haydn was often with us — & express'd much pleasure, when my beloved mother took the upper part (with me) of a Duett of Handels (in his fine Opera of Poro) — She had a fine high soprano voice — & had been (when very young) a scholar of the famous Geminiani. Given into my hands by my dear Mother, Fanny H. Henslowe [*sic*].' (The last sentence seems to have been added by Cecilia Maria's daughter.) Barthélemon lived at No. 8 Kennington Place, Vauxhall. See also Pohl, H. in L, p. 199.

P. 505: Paragraph 4 should begin: 'On St. Catherine's Day . . .' (not Catharine).

P. 506: List of second London Symphonies. Under *First Performance* of No. 104 add at beginning: '13th April 1795 (?) or 4th May (?) . . .'.

P. 508: Under First Concert. Dussek's new piano Concerto was probably the 'Second Grand Concerto in F' published by Corri & Dussek in 1794; see *infra*, *addendum* to p. 546.

P. 511: Last line of *Morning Chronicle* criticism; presumably the writer meant 'of Haydn, astonishing[,] inexhaustible . . .', *etc.*

P. 529: Section in large print towards bottom of page, line 1: delete whole sentence. I have since studied the diary in autograph (Mozarteum, Salzburg). Engl, who made ghastly mistakes in transcription throughout, reads 'Ich lernte in Canterbury den Famore, mahler keñen'. But what Haydn wrote was 'Ich lernte lauterburg den Famosen mahler keñen', *i. e.* I met Lauterburg, the famous painter. (Philipp Jakob Loutherbourg, 1740–1812, who had lived in England since 1771; he sketched Haydn's portrait.)

P. 533: Five lines from the bottom, remove period after word 'by'.

P. 541: Line 7, after the first name ('Leanders') add: '[*sc.* Leander]'; obviously the horn player so often listed in the London concerts is meant.

P. 546: Haydn's benefit concert (4th May 1795): Although the contemporary newspapers do not have a detailed programme, Mr. Albi Rosenthal of Oxford owns the hand-bill to this concert — the only one of a Haydn-Salomon concert known to exist today. The hand-bill is printed on one side of a tall folio sheet, and includes the texts of all the vocal numbers given, as a result of which the very complicated history of the Duet (sung by Morichelli and Morelli) can be solved. Before proceeding to the Duet, we should like to point out that Mr. Rosenthal's document is enhanced by a number of comments which someone — possibly a critic — penned on the margins: of the 'Military' Symphony, for example, the writer notes 'grand, but very noisy'. These amusing comments also reveal something of the way in which Haydn performed his London Symphonies: the *forte* passages were certainly not played in the wilting orchestral *mezzo forte* favoured by some modern conductors, who apparently think that music before Beethoven was never very loud.

Let us begin with the entry in Haydn's diary, which has been preserved only in Griesinger's biography. I have again examined the passage in question, and while the German punctuation leaves some doubt, it now seems to me that line 3 ought to read as follows: '(Rovedino); Concerto (Ferlandy) for the first time; Duet (Morichelli and Morelli) by me . . .'; in other words, it was the Concerto and not the Duet which was played 'for the first time'. The point is significant in view of that which follows.

Haydn's opera, *Orlando Paladino* (1782), includes a Duet between Eurilla and Pasquale on the text, 'Quel tuo visetto amabile' (B flat, 2–4). Apparently the piece soon became very popular as a separate number, for it was printed in piano-vocal score by Torricella (copy in the Library of Congress, Washington)[1] and circulated in manuscript copies: the Paris Conservatoire owns a *MS.* score on which the work is listed as having been performed at the Teatro S. Moisè, Venice, in 1794. When Haydn went to England, he seems to have taken the Duet with him, for when the Italian opera at King's Theatre staged Da Ponte's *Il burbero di buon*

---

[1] M.1552, A.2. H.2. The title, in an ornate frame, reads: 'Duette Airs / Quel tuo visetto amabile &c. / Composée et accomodée / pour Le Clavecin / Par Mr Ios. Haydn / Dedièe [*sic*] / A. Son Altesse Madame la Princesse / Charlotte Leihnowsky / nee Comtesse Althan / par son tres humble et tres obeissant / Serviteur Christoph Toricella . . . Publièe [*sic*] et se vend a Vienne chez Christoph Toricella'. Thus it would seem that Haydn also made the piano reduction.

cuore on 17th May 1794, the performance included Haydn's Duet as one of the inserted numbers, but with a new text, 'Quel cor umano e tenero'. The opera was given with additional music by 'Haydn, Trento and G. C. Ferrari', and the *Oracle*, writing of the performance, says: '. . . Of the music, what was in the best possible style was a Duo between Morelli and Morichelli, written by the excellent Haydn'.[1] The new version was printed in full score by Corri and Dussek.[2] In a copy of Dussek's '[Second] Grand Concerto in F . . . as Performed at the Professional [and] Salomon's Concerts [and] King's Theatre, Haymarket' (BM, g. 452. [9]), Corri and Dussek print their newest catalogue, in which, under 'New Vocal Music Opera Songs' of 1794, 'Haydens Duetto' is listed at 3 shillings.

Now one would have expected that the performance of the Duet at Haydn's benefit concert in 1795 would have followed the new text; but the hand-bill shows us that Haydn reverted to the original words, 'Quel tuo visetto': music is always best suited to the words for which it is originally composed, and Haydn probably felt that his Duet was best served by 'Quel tuo visetto' and not by 'Quel cor umano e tenero'.

P. 551: Text under illustration, line 2: For 'British Museum [*etc.*]' read 'Library of Congress, Washington'. The BM document concerns the rights of the first six Salomon Symphonies, not the last six.

P. 553: Last paragraph, line 3: For '1788' read '1789'.

P. 554: N. 4: Add the following sentence: 'But it can also refer to No. 92, which was probably played in the 1791 series (*cf.* Hoboken Cat., p. 175)'.

P. 557: N. 8: Add: 'Meanwhile I have shown this work to be by Friedrich Witt: see 'The *Jena* Symphony', MUSIC REVIEW XVIII/2 (May 1957)'.

P. 559, lines 2–3. Haydn was in Eisenstadt during the Summer (see his letter to Luigia Polzelli, dated 21st June); although he bought the house at Gumpendorf, he immediately set about having it enlarged and remodelled and did not actually settle there till after his second return from London in the Summer of 1795.

P. 560: Last paragraph: Professor J. P. Larsen recently discovered the only complete copy of Haydn's *L'anima del filosofo* among the uncatalogued music in the Paris Conservatoire. Although I could only briefly examine the manuscript (a photograph is in the archives of the Joseph Haydn Institut, Cologne), I am able to state that our proposed chronological order has proved to be correct. The Paris source, which is in four volumes, includes one *secco* which we did not have — linking the Death Scene of Euridice (ending in E flat) with the D major beginning of Orfeo's big *scena*, in the Second Act. The *MS.* also includes the Overture (see

---

[1] See A. Loewenberg, 'Lorenzo da Ponte in London', MUSIC REVIEW, IV/3 (August 1943), pp. 177 *f.* and *Annals of Opera*, 2nd ed., p. 546.

[2] Copy in the Esterházy Archives, Budapest, from Haydn's own collection. Dr. A. van Hoboken kindly provided me with a microfilm of the print.

also p. 566). Despite this evidence, I do not believe that the Overture was written originally for *Orfeo*, but that Haydn, wanting to make his opera available for performances, simply inserted it later so that the work would have a proper beginning.

P. 566: Paragraph 2: see *supra*, p. 560.

Concerning Section 3 (pp. 566 *ff.*), 'Melodic Origins . . .", a good deal remains to be said. Certain critics seem to think that because I believe Kuhač's theory as to the folk-song origin of certain of Haydn's melodies, I am again trying to prove that Haydn was a Croatian. Anyone who has studied E. F. Schmid's authoritative work on the subject,[1] however, must know that Haydn came of German-speaking peasant stock, and that he had no Croatian, Hungarian, Gipsy or Slavonic blood in his veins. But no amount of philistine chauvinism and no attempts to besmirch Kuhač (whether his name was originally Koch or not) will, I fear, alter the profoundly Slavonic character of some of Haydn's melodies. We must qualify the *amount* of melodies in which such Eastern European elements are predominant: they represent but a fraction of his total output and are always a deliberate 'exotic excursion' (if I may borrow the excellent term from my colleague, Professor Bence Szabolcsi, whose extensive paper on 'Haydn and the National Folk-Song of Hungary'[2] was read at the Haydn Congress in Budapest in 1959). The point is that these Eastern elements are clearly apparent in several of Haydn's London Symphonies; it is also curious that the Trio in G for pianoforte, violin and cello (Larsen No. 25; B. & H. and Peters No. 1), which contains the famous 'Rondo in the gipsy style', was written in England. And in the case of the 'Gipsy Rondo', Haydn's source — which definitely predates the trio — has been discovered.[3] The reason for this sudden appearance of Slavonic folk-melodies in Haydn's London period is not, I think, as mysterious as might at first be thought: probably the English public had had very little opportunity to hear this 'exotic' music, and when Haydn tried it out, he found that it was very popular with the 'nobility and gentry' and then proceeded to repeat the mixture as before.

The trouble with all scientific research into the folk-melodies of Haydn's time is that almost nothing was written down. Kuhač's enemies — and they extend from Germany and Austria to East Forty-Third Street in New York City — will thus contend: the peasants took the melodies from Haydn. Leaving aside the chronological question for a moment, it is quite obvious to anyone familiar with Eastern European folk-music that the beginning of Symphony No. 103/II (*cf.* Ex. 1, p. 568), with its sequence g-c-e♭-f♯-g, is profoundly *osteuropäisch*: Zoltán Kodály, with whom this part of the book formed a recent discussion in Budapest, says it is

---

[1] *Joseph Haydn, Ein Buch von Vorfahren und Heimat des Meisters*, Kassel, 1934.

[2] I am grateful to Professor Szabolcsi for letting me read this paper on the occasion of a recent research trip to Budapest (Autumn 1958).

[3] I refer to Professor Szabolcsi's paper.

Hungarian; the Turks say it is Turkish; the Poles, Polish; and Kuhač maintains that it is Croatian. Actually, it is all of that; for the melodic line is the common property of all Eastern European peoples. It is very doubtful if we shall ever find an old dated manuscript from which we can prove that Haydn did in fact use an old folk-tune as the basis for the Symphony; but the fact of the tune's Slavonic character is clear and incontrovertible.

The next point concerns melodies which Kuhač maintains are Croatian, but which do not have any particularly strong Eastern European flavour: the opening of Symphony No. 103/IV (*cf.* p. 568, Ex. 1e) is of this sort. Whereas the very notes of Ex. 1a are Slavonic in character, neither the notes nor the melodic curve of Ex. 1e are necessarily based on a folk-tune; on the contrary, they appear to be a typical product of Haydn's own late-period style — one of those melodies which are ideally fitted for motivic development (the ♩ ♩ ♩ ♩ |♩ ♩ is the kind of figure which is pregnant with rhythmic possibilities, and one which is characteristic of all Haydn's music). Here, the possibility of the Croatian peasants having borrowed Haydn's tune and adapted it for their needs does not seem as impossible as in the case of No. 103/II. Recently, Mr. Fritz Spiegl drew my attention to the fact that at least three mechanical organs known to him contain the tune, slightly altered in certain small details, of the finale of Haydn's Symphony No. 100 in G ('Military' — 1794). This was of course very exciting news: the little organs usually entitled the tune 'Lord Cathcart' or 'Cathcart', and armed with this information, I sent the whole evidence to Mr. A. Hyatt King of the British Museum, who passed it on to the English Folk Dance and Song Society. Mr. S. Jackson, the Society's Librarian, writes as follows:

'. . . I have found "Lord Cathcart" as a country dance in two collections; and also the tune in one of our nineteenth-century *MS.* tune books. Details as follows:

LORD CATHCART —

as LORD CATHCART'S WELCOME in *Treasures of Terpsichore* . . . being a Collection of all the most popular Country Dances . . . together with all the new Dances for 1809. By T. Wilson, London, 1809.

as LORD CATHCART'S WELCOME TO SCOTLAND in *Wheatstone's Selection* of Elegant and Fashionable Country Dances, Reels, Waltzs [*sic*], *etc.* for the Ensuing Season, with an Accompt. for the Piano Forte or Harp by Augs. Voigt, *etc.* Sold by C. Mitchell, at his Musical Circulating Library and Instrument Ware rooms, 51, Southampton Row, Russel [*sic*] Sqre. (*n.d.*, but between 1808–1814).

as LORD CATHCART in a manuscript book of country dance tunes, *etc.* which is not earlier than the first decade or so of the nineteenth century.

Lord Cathcart is presumably Sir William Shaw, tenth Baron Cathcart, and first Viscount and Earl Cathcart (1755–1843) who after a distinguished military career was created Viscount Cathcart in 1807 and appointed C. in C. Scotland presumably in the same year.

. . . It does seem . . . that the country dance, and country dance tune, "Lord Cathcart" did not appear before about 1808 . . . . At present it seems that "Lord Cathcart" is derived from Haydn's melody rather than vice versa'.

Last Spring (1958), I was examining a pile of anonymous music in the shop of Mr. Hermann Baron, London, to whom I am indebted for many kindnesses. In an incomplete *MS.* of songs, *etc.* I found an old copy of 'Lord Cathcart's Wee' (as it is entitled on the *MS.*), which Mr. Baron very kindly presented to me. A photograph of the dance is shown overleaf. The paper on which the *MS.* is written is English in origin and contains the dated watermark '1807'.

Here, then, would seem to be strong evidence that the tunes of Haydn's works actually made their way into the world not only in the concert hall but, arranged as dances, in the parlour and ball-room. The fact is not surprising if we remember that Mozart's *Figaro* became so popular in Prague that when Mozart arrived there to produce *Don Giovanni* he was delighted to hear his *Figaro* arranged as dance music. In fact, he himself arranged 'Non più andrai' as a Country Dance (K.609, no. 1).

Having shown how the situation works, as it were, in reverse, we can also demonstrate at least one case (apart from that of the 'Gipsy Rondo' mentioned above) in which written evidence supports the Kuhač theory.

P. 264, Ex. 21 and p. 351, Ex. 3g list a melody which Haydn used at least twice, in an early *Divertimento* (*c.* 1761) and in Symphony No. 60 (1774); the first part of the tune also appears in the Sextet in E flat for 2 horns and strings (original and authentic version of the Quartet Op. 2, No. 3). I proposed that it was a 'favourite Slavonic melody' (p. 353), but I never expected to find any written evidence of my supposition. In 1957, however, while on a research trip through Southern Germany, I examined the music archives in the Monastery of Metten, on the Danube. The archives were in a state of indescribable confusion, as is unfortunately the case in many Austrian and German monasteries after World War II, and there was no opportunity to copy anything properly, since it was late in a winter's afternoon and there were no electric lights in the room where the music was kept. In a pile of early eighteenth-century concerti (Wagenseil, Hofmann, *etc*) I came across a very early and curious manuscript for violin solo consisting of three little anonymous pieces, one of which turned out to be the melody in question. There was no possibility of having the little manuscript photographed, and when, in 1959, the Metten Library was reorganized, there seemed little hope that we would ever find the uncatalogued sheet again. I returned to Metten in the late Winter of 1959, however, and went through all the anonymous manuscripts, sheet by sheet; as if by a miracle, the oblong double sheet turned up again, and the monks there kindly arranged to have it microfilmed. The melody Haydn used — it is entitled 'Der Nachtwachter' [*sic*], 'The Night Watchman' — is herewith reproduced in facsimile in its entirety. Interested readers will thus be able to compare Haydn's setting with the one at Metten which, though the paper and watermark do not admit of a precise date, is definitely eighteenth century and thus contemporary with Haydn's adaptations. This curious discovery of an eighteenth-century source of one of the folk-songs Haydn used shows that we may yet turn up considerably more information about the origins of Haydn's Eastern European melodies than we had hitherto dared to hope.

P. 569: Line 1: Read '1939, p. 4 . . .'.

P. 569: Line 6: Read '. . . cites the cry as "Red Hot Buns" . . .' (not 'Hot Cross Buns').

P. 573: Concerning the slow introductions in the tonic minor, Dr. Roger Fiske points out that tonic minor *Adagio* introductions, especially in the key of D minor, were very popular with English composers of the year 1794; Dr. Fiske considers it likely that the introductions of Haydn's Symphonies Nos. 101 and 104 derive their particular musical language from similar *Adagios* in English music of the period. Chronologically, too, Dr. Fiske is able to prove that the English works precede Haydn's. We know altogether far too little about the English music being produced during Haydn's London visits, and we hope that Dr. Fiske, who is an acknowledged expert, will throw some much-needed light on this subject.

P. 579: Third music ex — add *fz* under first note of last bar.

'Lord Cathcart's Wee'

From a contemporary manuscript in the author's collection

P. 597: In list of Masses at the bottom of the page: The autograph of the *Missa* ('Schöpfungsmesse') was unknown to my friend and colleague, Professor Larsen, and when I brought it to his attention, he persuaded Herr G. Henle to purchase the manuscript; subsequently, the autograph was donated to the Bavarian State Library (1956).

APPENDICES

General Remarks: With the appearance of Hoboken's Catalogue, part of the appendices' *raison d'être* has ceased to exist, especially in that which concerns the printed sources. On the other hand, the evaluation of the sources, and the detailed description of the manuscripts may continue to be of some use to musicians and scholars. Thus I shall include, in the forthcoming list, additional manuscripts, but only in so far as they are missing both in Hoboken and in my book. In particular, I have since uncovered a substantial number of *MS.* sources confirming the correct or probable authors of the symphonies listed in Appendix II, and these sources may be of use to scholars doing research in the fields of eighteenth-century symphonists apart from Haydn. I have not listed under the *corrigenda* the more exact dates for printed editions which Hoboken has been able to include, partly as a result of Cari Johansson's magnificent research into French publishers of the period, and partly by a number of hitherto unknown publishers' announcements.

The three principal collections of *MS.* sources to Haydn's symphonies which are not evaluated in my book are: (1) the so-called 'Frankfurt Collection', which Ewald Lassen recently discovered in the Frankfurt-am-Main Stadtbibliothek, despite constant attempts on the part of the library and its musical director ('the *MSS.* cannot be of much value, since they are of known works') to prevent him from doing so. I have included the three *MS.* copies which are positively authentic, and written on Esterházy paper (see *supra*, p. 34); and also some important *corrigenda* to the Frankfurt sources in Appendix II; but a full evaluation of the collection's importance, textually and otherwise, must await the detailed publication which Mr. Lassen is now preparing. (2) The Haydn collection in the archives of the Palacio Real in Madrid, which Professor Jan LaRue brought to light in 1956. I have included one or two interesting points from this large collection, but its proper evaluation, too, must be made at a later date. (3) The Haydn sources in Czechoslovakia. In 1959, I was able to make a trip to Czechoslovakia; but the results arrived too late for inclusion in the *Music Review*, and I have included them above (see p. 27) in a special section.

APPENDIX I

Pp. 612 *f.*: No. 22 is not 'MA' but 'AM' and was produced by the North Italian paper mill of Andrea Mattizzoli. The 'GF', 'GV' and 'GFA' papers are probably all from the mill of Galvani Fratelli in Pordenone. See Jan LaRue, 'Die Datierung

NEW ROOM, KING's THEATRE.

Dr. HAYDN's Night.

MONDAY, May 4, 1795.

very good —
nothing —

PART I.

Overture, MS.	Haydn.
Song, Sig. Rovedino,	Ferrari.
Concerto Hautbois, Sig. Ferlendis, from Venice, (being his First Performance in this Country)	Ferlendis.
Duetto, Madame Morichelli and Sig. Morelli,	Haydn.
New Overture, *very noisy*	Ditto.

Astonishing fine command of the Instrument, but degenerated into mere foolish trick

PART II.

Military Symphony,	Haydn.
Song, Madame Morichelli,	Paisiello.
Concerto Violin, Mr. Viotti,	
New Scene, Madame Banti,	Haydn.

(Grand but very noisy
Most delicate execution, but very little music in the composition

FINALE.

Song, Sig. Rovedino.—*Ferrari.*

RECITATIVE.

Or dell' avversa forte amata Berenice,
Più non mi lagno, e sprezza le minaccie
Eil rigor di tua fede
Si' Caro e del tuo Amore,
Ma quel di tua vittoria
Orgoglioso Alessandro
Importuna tristezza scena la gioja
E adombra qual mai, nube di duol
L' alma t' ingombra! Tu impallidisci
A forza trattieni il pianto
Affoghi nel tuo petto i Sospiri
Tu folgore di Marte, della Grecia ferror
S' angi e s' adiri, in tal flato
A rendermi infelice io sfido il fato,
Tu m' involasti un regno
Hai di trionfo il vanto
Ma tu mi cedi intanto
L' Impero di quel cor,
Ci esamini il sembiante
Dica ogni fido Amante
Chi più d' invidia e degno
Se il vinto, o il vincitor.

DUETTO, M. Morichelli and Sig. Morelli.
Haydn.

Eurina.
Quel tuo visetto Amabile
Proprio mi fa languir,
Sento nel petto un spasimo
Che non lo fo zittir
Ma ta furbetto e graziosetto
Ben lo comprendi meglio,
L' intendi che voglio dir
Tu lospiri tu rimiri
Mi vuoi bene non tasda.

Pasquale.
Ah eh ih oh uh,
Il cavolo ed il Padrone,
Per amor in conclusione,
Non di possano fresar.

Eurina.
Per amor in conclusione,
Più mi sento ad Infiamar.

Morelli's short part diverting in the buffo style.

Song, Madame Morichelli.—*Paisiello.*

RECITATIVE.

Crudele, or colei piangi
Che spingesti tu stessa a si tragico fin!
Misera Dafne, ma più misero Alceo!
Tutto perdesti, che ti resta a sperar!
Con' il destino amista
Ingannator cangiò d' aspetto!
Questo è il piacere, questo il contento
Ahi lasso, che ad Alceo promettesti
Amore, Apollo, numi tutti del Ciel
Che in tronco, in suffo, in erma,
Alpestra rupe!
Per pietà' mi trasforma
Etu follievo d' un disperato cor
Perchè non vieni, morte,
Il corso a troncar de mali miei
Ahi! meco sei tanto crudel tu sei
Ho perduto il bel sembiante
Nò non trovo alcun ristoro
Ho perduto il mio tesoro
La mia ninfa, oh dio dov' è.
Quelli monti, e quelle piante
Sempre udranno i miei lamenti
Chi mai vide tra i viventi
Sventurata al par di me.
Dafne mia felice amante
Vissi ogn' ora a te d' appresso
Odio or tutto, odio me stesso
Che diviti io fon da te.

Nothing more than a decent second opera singer

NEW SCENE, Madame Banti.—*Haydn.*

RECITATIVE.

Berenice che fai!
Mori il tuo bene
Stupida, e tu non corri
Oh di d' recilla l' incerto passo
Un gelido mi scote
Insolito tremor tutte le vene
Ea gran pena il suo peso il piè sostiene
Dove son' quali confuta folla d' idee
Tutte funeste adombra
La mia ragion, Veggo Demetrio' Il veggo
Che in atto di ferir— tersmati vivi
D' antigono io farò del core
Ad onta vohu a giurarglì sè
Dirò che l' amo misera mè
S' oscura il giorno balena il Ciel'
L' anno irritato, i miei meditati sospiri
Ahinè lasciate ch' io Soccorra il mio ben
Barbari Dei voi m' impedite
E intanto forse un colpo improviso
Ah farete contenti. Eccolo ucciso
Aspetta, anima bella ombre compagne
A Lete andrem se non potei salvarti
Porrò fedel, ma tu mi guardi, e parti
Non parte bell' idol mio
Per quell' onda
All' altra sponda
Voglio anch' io passar con te
Me infelice che fingo! Che ragioso!
Dove repita sono
Dal torrente crudel de miei martiri
Misera Berince ah tu deliri
Perchè se tanti siete
Che delirar mi fate
Perchè non m' uccidete
Affanni del mio cor
Conforte od Dio crefsete
Finche mi paiga ata
Con toglierna la vita
L' eccelso del dolor.

Recitative very finely expressed

Something of pleasing air

Recitative I think

Ends with an air in the minor Key.

Banti has a clear, sweet, equable voice, her low & high notes equally good. Her recitative admirably expressive. Her voice rather wants fulness of tone; her shake is weak & imperfect.

☞ The Subscribers to the Opera Concert are respectfully informed, that the two remaining Subscription Concerts will be on the 11th and 18th of next Month, (the 25th being Whit-Monday.

⁂ At the request of a very great number of the Subscribers, there will be Two additional Concerts upon *Wednesday*, the 27th of May, and *Wednesday*, the 3d of June, (the Concert of Ancient Music being over on the 20th of May) for which nights two separate Tickets will be delivered for *One Guinea*; and the Subscribers to this Concert will have a preference for themselves and their friends until the 18th of May, after which the Subscription will be open for the Public. At these Concerts Mr. FERLENDIS, from Venice, will play (for the first time in this country) upon the English Horn.

Hand-bill for Haydn's Benefit Concert in 1795 (Albi Rosenthal, London — Oxford).

The first two pages of music of the recently discovered autograph of Haydn's 'Oxford' Symphony (No. 92). Paris, Bibliothèque Nationale.

von Wasserzeichen im 18. Jahrhundert' (Vienna Musicological Congress, 1956: 'Beispiele', p. 3). No. 22 and No. 62: for 'half-cup' read 'bow'. The 'C' found in many Italian watermarks means 'Cartelleria' (paper mill).

P. 614: Group VI: Probably paper from the mill of I. G. Zug in Lower Austria. Group VIII (title — read: 'German paper mills, mostly at Wolfegg, Augsburg and Nürnberg'. Nos. 4 and 6 from the mill of Johann Anton Unold, Wolfegg. Nos. 9–14 from the mill of Johann Christoph Bernhaupt, Simmelsdorf (Nürnberg).

P. 615: Source 5, line 5: Read ' "AST" — *cf.* No. 3, source 4 . . .'.

P. 616 (Symphony No. 2): Add source (2a) *MS.* parts, Kremsmünster, cat. H 38, 34; title-page lost; pts. for 2 ob., 2 cor., str. Two copyists: (a) vln. I, II; (b) Frater Kramel, who made the other pts. 4° paper from Kremsmünster paper mill (watermarks: letters 'IAW' on one part of the sheet, an eagle on the other). An important early source, probably the *MS.* on which (1) was based: the reverse is unlikely, because the present parts do not duplicate Lambach's inconsistencies, *e. g.* I, bar 6 (see *infra*). Source of local origin, *c.* 1760–1768.

P. 624 *ff.*: Pts. of Nos. 6–8 from what we believe to be the former Kees Collection are in the Monastery of St. Peter, Salzburg (see *supra*, p. 38). No title-page extant. The title at the head of each part generally reads: 'Tre / Sinfonie, Conctz / Del Sig: Jos: Haydn [red ink: 'N° 80.81.82'] Le Matin Le Midi Le Soir'. 'Sinfonia LXXX' *etc.* (see p. 38). For each Symphony there are 3 vln. I, 3 vln. II, 2 vla., 2 *basso* and one each of the other pts. 4° brownish paper, probably of Viennese origin, end of the eighteenth century.

P. 633: Source 4: I have since restored the false title to its proper file. The wind parts of No. 12 are missing.

P. 635: Source 8: No oboe parts.

P. 641: Under date of comp., Symphony No. 17, 'Earliest ref.' add 'Moravian Church Archives, Winston-Salem, North Carolina — dated 1766. The *MS.* parts, made by the Moravian composer J. F. Peter, include 2 ob., 2 cor., str.'.

P. 651: Symphony No. 23: Under 'Cat. ref.' last entry, for 'parts lost' read 'fragments extant'.

P. 658: Source 8: For '1769' read '1786'. See Martha Bruckner, 'Eine unbekannte Haydn-Sinfonie' (in: *Mitteilungen aus dem Baron Brukenthalischen Museum* XI [1946], pp. 8 *ff.*).

P. 662 (Symphony No. 30): Add correction to G.A. — 2nd movt., bar 1, V. I, II 4th note c".

P. 665: Add † to No. 33 (MGM Records, U.S.A.).

P. 669 (Symphony No. 35): Source 16: The first horn part of the Welcker print has a simplified reading in the recapitulation (where in the original the horn plays a run up to g' or g", depending on whether *alto* or *basso* is meant; in view of the

4

simplification, it would seem that the part was regarded as *alto*, because the run is not at all difficult if played *basso*).

P. 671: 3 lines from bottom, at cat. no. '22' to Regensburg source.

P. 674: The Library of Congress has an early copy of the Symphony under anonymous (the title-page must have become separated from the parts): M.1001, A. (9), with pts. on 4° paper (watermarks illegible) for 2 ob., 2 cor., str.

P. 678: Source 13: The Sieber print can be dated 1771 (not 1773), and thus Hummel reprinted from Sieber and not vice versa.

P. 679: Source 1, line 3: At beginning of sentence read '2nd movt., meas. 45 . . .' (not 1st movt.).

P. 681: Add new source, of Viennese origin, in archives of the Heilig-Kreuz-Kirche, Augsburg (textually a very valuable and early source).

P. 683, under Critical edition: Add 'Eulenburg No. 544 (Landon), based on (1), (2), &c.'.

P. 686: Source 17: Copy of this important and extremely rare print in University Library at Lund, Sweden (Cat. Wenster's don: B-4).

P. 689: Add new source, of local origin, in the archives Heilig-Kreuz-Kirche, Augsburg; 2 clarini pts. in a somewhat later hand; no timp. pt.

P. 694: Symphony No. 53: The title 'L'impériale' first appears in Sieber's Thematic Catalogue of Haydn's Symphonies.

P. 696: Source 8: The fag. part is lost. Perfs. on cover from '3 Martii 1783' to 1868 (!).

P. 699: Symphony No. 55: Add new source, of local origin, in the archives of the Heilig-Kreuz-Kirche, Augsburg.

P. 700 (Symphony No. 55): The first edition is missing in my book. It is a print by Guera of Lyon, a publisher whose prints are extremely scarce and about whom we know very little. Although I have not as a rule mentioned the prints missing in my book, since they are all in Hoboken's Catalogue, I feel that readers may wish to consult these rare Guera prints, all of which are in the Cambridge University Library, some from the Marion Scott Coll., some from other sources. The Cambridge copies also contain Guera's catalogues in various stages. Hoboken has this Guera print listed under Symphony No. 43, the *incipit* of which begins similarly but is, I assure my readers, not the work which M. Guera printed. This is particularly amusing in view of the ponderous footnote in which poor Gerber is accused of confusing Nos. 43 and 55: the confusion, I fear, is chronologically this side of the *Neues historisch-biographisches Lexikon der Tonkünstler*. The Cat. no. of the Guera print of No. 55 (issued with a Symphony by Lochon, in E flat, and one by Vaňhal, in F) in the Cambridge University Library is 4784.

P. 701: Symphony No. 57: Under Cat. ref., after Göttweig, add '(fragments of the parts extant)'. Add †(recording by Philips).

P. 703: Source 3, line 2: Read '. . . Viola / e / . . . Heydn . . .'

P. 705: Date of comp. — 1774 (see *supra*, p. 349).

P. 706: Source 14: Add 'Ad usum / Fidelis Candon [Landon?]' — *cf.* No. 71, source 2.

P. 706: Source 24 is Guera (Lyon) and Boyer (Paris): the Pichl Symphony is App. II, No. 72.

P. 706: Symphony No. 61, Source 1: Title-page (otherwise blank): 'Sinfonia'; underneath this, in another hand, 'Haydn'; p. 2 (first p. of music) 'In Nomine Domini . . . [*etc.*]'. There are 80 pp. (40 sheets), not 40 pp.

P. 707: Source 9: Copy in Donaueschingen; no timpani part.

P. 708: Source 5: Read '4° Austrian (?) paper (watermarks: illegible) . . .'. Fag. missing.

P. 708: Source 19: Add at end: A late *MS.* score of this version, without the finale, in BM, Add. 31708 (No. 4).

P. 709: Under *incipits*: For 'IV' read 'IV*a*' and for 'IV*a*' read 'IV*b*'.

P. 709: Under Cat. ref., Göttweig: For 'parts lost' read 'fragments extant'.

P. 710: Line 5: Add 'Fl. and fag. parts *tacent* after III'.

P. 710: Source 1, line 2: At end of line, read: ' — the latter occur only in vla. pt., which may be a later substitute for the original pt.); source of Viennese origin . . .' (*etc.*). See also p. 41: these pts. were owned by F. X. Glöggl, and his initials are on the title-page.

P. 713: Under Cat. ref.: After Göttweig, for 'parts lost' read 'pts. extant' and add (2*a*) under sources, *MS.* pts., Göttweig.

P. 716: Source 3: It is doubtful whether these parts ever existed (despite Artaria-Botstiber); they are in no Artaria catalogue, and no copy exists. Artaria published only (4) as far as we know.

P. 718: Source 8: The Minuet = No. 62/III.

P. 718: Source 20: No Minuet.

P. 718 (Symphony No. 71): Under list of movts. 'II' add 'erroneously in DKE as IX, F–4'.

P. 720: Under scoring: Madrid (Palacio Real, ms. 628) has a *MS.* with the GdM scoring, including timp.

P. 721 (add correction to pp. 385 *ff.*): The following correction — which is a very important one — could be made only as a result of a recent trip to the Esterházy Archives in Budapest. Again I learned the sad fact that one cannot, in musicology (as in any science), trust anyone, any fact, or any tradition: everything must be verified. We read *inter alia* in Geiringer, Hoboken and Landon (p. 385) about the Symphony No. 73 and how its Finale was taken from Act III of *La fedeltà premiata* (performed at Esterháza Castle in 1780). This is not the case. None of these gentlemen took the trouble to consult the original score or libretto, and in Hoboken's Catalogue we are even given a description of the beginning of Act III of which not a word is true.

The autograph score of *La fedeltà premiata* is preserved largely in the Esterházy Archives (Act III is entirely wanting) — Ms. Mus. I, Nr. 6 — and an original libretto for the revival of 1782 at Esterháza is also there — Mus. th. 2314-C. The autograph includes the fine movement later used as the Finale to the Symphony *La Chasse*, but it is obvious, when one examines the score, that the piece was used as the Overture to *Act I* of the Opera, not as the Prelude to Act III. The score begins with the title-page: 'Opera' (Haydn's hand) 'la Fedeltà premiata' (another hand) and the 'Bogen' (sets of usually four double sheets) are numbered in Haydn's hand: 'Bogen' Nos. 1–4 are *La Chasse*, 'Bogen' 5 is the beginning of *Atto primo*.

P. 721: Source 2: Cancel the whole entry and read: Autograph, EH, as Overture to *La fedeltà premiata*, Act I, Cat. Ms. Mus. I, 6. Including the title-page and two blank pages, there are 16 sheets, or 32 pp., the last two of which are also blank. Title (*not* 'La Chasse'): 'In Nomine Domini di me giuseppe Haydn mp. $\overline{780}$'. Instruments: '2 Trombe / o / 2 Corni / in D‖Tympani / in D‖oboe / 1‖2do‖Flauto‖ Fagotti‖Violi[no] / 1‖2do‖ Viola [below this, and later crossed out, is the word "Violoncello"]‖Bassi'. Oblong, ten-stave paper, 31.5×23 cm. (watermarks: I, 1, 12). At end of *MS.*: 'Attaca / Subito il Coro', referring to No. 1 of the actual opera. Originally there was no double bar (it being an Overture), but Haydn later drew one across the whole score at bar 80.

P. 721: Source 3: The mystery of the 'lost' autograph of the clavier arrangement is, I think, solved by a *MS.* in the GdM: a piano reduction of the work which is listed as an autograph but is not. This is no doubt the manuscript to which Artaria-Botstiber (p. 26) refer.

P. 721: Source 4: The signature on the BM copy is definitely *not* by Haydn, as anyone even faintly conversant with Haydn's handwriting can see at once: unfortunately, I relied on the (otherwise trustworthy) BM Catalogue and did not examine the actual source until after the book had gone to press. I managed to correct this mistake in the *Union Catalogue* at the very last minute (thanks to the energetic action of Mr. O. W. Neighbour), but the error is unfortunately in Hoboken.

P. 723 (Symphony No. 75): Under Scoring: Timp. also in *MS.* 641 of the Palacio Real Archives, Madrid.

P. 725 (Symphony No. 76): Under Date of comp., see *erratum*, p. 388.

P. 725: Source 2: Penultimate line should begin — 'small, oblong "Postpapier" (paper used for mailing) with watermarks "EC" and letter "R" with pillars on each side', make change also for Nos. 77 (2) and 78 (2).

P. 726: Source 15: The Torricella print is now known to be authentic and should be moved up to category, *Authentic Prints*: an announcement of Torricella's new Haydn *opus* in the *Wiener Zeitung* of 7th July 1784, reads '3 letzte Sinfonien, von ihm selbst korrigiert'.

P. 729 (Secondary *MSS.*): Add Heilig-Kreuz-Kirche Archives, Augsburg (local copy).

P. 731 (Symphony No. 80, Secondary *MSS.*): Add *MS.* pts., Eferding (Fürstl. Starhemberg'sche Bibliothek). The very rare Guera print of Symphonies Nos. 80, 81 and Ordoñez' Symphony in C — missing in my book, but see Hoboken — is possibly the first edition of all three works; a copy is in the Marion Scott Collection, Cambridge University Library (Cat. 106 a–i). (See comment above to p. 700.)

P. 732 (Symphony No. 82): Source 2: The paper is again the small-sized 'Post-papier', paper for mailing; watermarks as in No. 76 (2) — see *corrigendum*, *supra*, p. 725, source 2.

Pp. 732 *ff.*: For all the Paris Symphonies (Nos. 82–87), please change the type of paper and watermark of the Forster *MSS.* (B. M. Egerton 2379) to read as in *corrigendum* to p. 732.

P. 734: Line 2: In the Hummel print, the bassoon pts. are omitted (!) and re-written in the vla. pt.

P. 735: Add source (2a) *MS.* parts by Johann (or Joseph, Jr.) Elssler, EH, cat. Ms. Mus. I, 89; pts. for 1 fl., 2 ob., 'Fagotti', 2 cor., 2 vln. I, 2 vln. II, 2 vla., vcl., cb. On the cb. pt., the *incipit* in Haydn's hand.

P. 735: Source 3: Strike out the last sentence; the *MS.* is apparently from Haydn's legacy, and was later owned by J. N. Hummel, Prince Esterházy's Kapellmeister (see Hoboken, pp. 289 and 405).

P. 736: Under Cat. ref., Göttweig: For 'parts lost' read 'fragments extant'.

P. 737: Under Sketches: (1) now owned by R. Aumann, Aarau (Switzerland) — the 1st p. reproduced on plate 88 of R. Aumann, *Die Handschrift der Künstler*, Bern 1953.

P. 744: The autograph of No. 92 has been rediscovered (see *supra*, pp. 28, 48, 428).

P. 754: Last music ex.: This proposed version is in fact that of the Monzani and Cimador print (= Birchall).

P. 759: r.h. column: 3, 31-lines 5–6 should read '. . . have *g* (*natural*), not *g sharp*, and ob. II, vln. II *e* (*natural*)'.

P. 771 (Symphony No. 101): Under nickname 'Clock': Read 'title from the late 18th cent. (Traeg published a piano arr. of the *Andante* as "Rondo . . . 'Die Uhr' " in 1798)'.

P. 774: Source 2: The Minuet is wanting in all the pts.

P. 776 (Symphony 'A'): Under Cat. ref., Göttweig: For 'parts lost' read 'vln. II rediscovered by author in 1957. The text shows a very close connection to that of the St. Florian pt. A new *MS.* source, with the wind pts., has been rediscovered by E. Lassen in the so-called 'Frankfurt Collection' (see *supra*, Appendices, General Remarks): in that source, the finale is written in 3/8 time (as against St. Florian and the very early Göttweig sources)'.

P. 787: The 'Frankfurt Collection' includes an old *MS.* of Symphony No. 33 *with the timpani part* which Mr. Ewald Lassen kindly copied out for me. The Frankfurt *MS.* also includes trumpet parts which are *not* identical with the horn parts. When in Prague, I was able to discover an early and important source of the Symphony (from the Clam Gallas Collection) which also contains the same trumpet and timpani parts. There is no question in my mind that they are genuine, and they are herewith included in their entirety. I am grateful to Mr. Lassen for sending me exact copies of the Frankfurt parts, which I could compare with those in Prague.

APPENDIX II

Note: To avoid double references, the following *addenda* refer in each case to the number of the Symphony, not the page number.

1: Add to Pichl (4) *MS.* source owned by Günther Rhau, with the title 'Pallas Dea' and *tempo Allegro con giusto*.

2: Hofmann's dates are 1738–1793 (see article in *MGG*).

3: (3), the authentic print contains 'Trois Simphonies' — copy in BM, g. 474.c.(7.).

4: Add to Haydn (3) *MS.* pts. Washington, M.1001,A2.K.65P. 'Del Sig^r G. Hayden'; on cover 'N° 6'. No timp.

6: *Tempo Allegro vivace* in many *MSS.* Add to Dittersdorf (7) *MS.* pts., Salzburg, St. Peter; (8) *MS.* pts., Donaueschingen, listed in thematic cat. of 1804 (parts= Mus. ms. 335).

7: *Tempo Allegro molto* in many *MSS.* Add to Hoffmeister (5) *MS.* pts., Basel, Cat. Kr. II 35; (6) *MS.* pts., Donaueschingen Mus. ms. 762.

8: Add to Haydn sources (10) printed pts., Bureau d'Abonnement Musical, Paris, *c.* 1775 (see App. I, No. 45, source 17) — *cf.* also Hoboken. The EH parts (as Vanhal) have the (*b*) sequence of movements, which is an interesting fact, I feel.

9: Add to Hofmann sources (5) Dunwalt Cat. 1770 [BM, Hirsch IV, 1081] — no trpts. and timp.

11 : Add to Haydn sources (4) *MS*. pts. Prague Nat. Mus. A. 31, dated 1774 (2 ob., 2 cor., str.). Add to Schneider's *data*: 1737–1812, organist (not *Regenschori*) at Melk.

14 : Add to Haydn sources (2) *MS*. pts. Basel, 'Six Symphonies N° 3'; (3) *MS*. pts. Basel, a second copy. Add to Sterkel: *MS*. pts. in Washington (M.1001, A.2.R.373) list 'Reichel' as the author, probably a bastardization of 'Sterkel'.

15 : Add to Haydn sources (4) *MS*. parts Madrid (Palacio Real), *MS*. 654.

17 : Add to Haydn (1) 'dated 1780'. Add to Guénin sources (3) printed pts., Schott, Mainz (pl. no. 153, *c.* 1793) — copy in Donaueschingen, Mus. Drwk. 1240.

18 : Add to scoring: Fl., 2 trpt., timp.

21 : Add to Hofmann (6) Dunwalt Cat. 1770 — *cf.* corr. to 9; (7) Sigmaringen Cat. 1766 (2 ob., 2 cor., 2 clarini, str.).

24 : Add †(Decca, cond. M. Wöldike). To scoring: one of St. Peter *MS*. also has timp. Add to Dittersdorf (9) — two sets of *MS*. pts. in St. Peter, one with timp. (11) printed pts., S. Markordt, Amsterdam, Op. I, No. 1 (copy in BM); (12) Sigmaringen Cat. 1766 — a later addition. *New edition* (as Dittersdorf) DTÖ 81 (XLIII/2), ed. V. Luithlen.

27 : *Incipit* II — *tempo* should be *Allegro assai*. Anton Zimmermann was Kapellmeister to Cardinal Batthianyi in Pressburg (see C. F. Pohl, *Denkschrift . . .* p. 19).

29 : Pleyel scoring includes 2 fag. (not 1), 2 trpt. and timp. Add to Haydn (2) *MS*. pts., Madrid Palacio Real, *MS*. 646. This again confirms the Spanish origin of the Washington Coll. Add to Pleyel sources (4) printed pts. Hummel, Berlin, Op. XXXI, Libro I (pl. no. 684); (5) Sarasin Cat., Basel.

33 : Add to Hofmann sources (2) in Kittel's Cat. of music at Detmold, 1780, as 'Hoffmann' (no christian name); (3) *MS*. pts., Berlin Hochschule, Cat. 1276.

34 : Under Haydn (3) read 'two *MS*. scores, one from Saltzmann Coll., Brussels'. Add to van Swieten (4) *MS*. score, Bst. (Marburg), 21586.

35 : Massoneau print in Kremsmünster is Cat. H 28, 236 (not H 28, 36).

37 : Add to Vaňhal sources (6) *MS*. pts., St. Peter, Salzburg, dated 1771 (*Allegro moderato*); (7) keyboard arr., Br. Cat. 1779–1780.

40 : Add to Vaňhal sources: (13) *MS*. pts., Michaelbeuern — incomplete — with no trpts. and timp.

42 : In *incipit* read ₵ for C. For 'Probable author' read 'Correct author'. Kloeffler was *Concertdirector* and also *Finanzassesor* at the Court of Bentheim-Steinfurt, Burg Steinfurt near Münster. An authentic source has been discovered at Rheda (Library of the Princes of Bentheim-Tecklenburg-Rheda, Province of Minden, Northern Germany): *MS*. pts., Cat. 698, the title-page autograph. A second set of pts., also at Rheda, is Cat. 903. (Information from Jan LaRue).

43: The Haydn parts (Zittau) are dated 6th November 1821.

44: Schmitt's dates are 1750–1815 (DTB, XXVIII); he went to Amsterdam about 1780, founded the publishing house of Schmitt there, and was in Frankfurt about 1803 (see Gerber, *Lexikon* 1812–1814). Add to Schmid source: Sigmaringen Cat. 1766 (no trpts., timp.). Add to Schmitt source: Dunwalt Cat. 1770 (*cf.* 9) — 2 cor., str. Probably Joseph Schmitt was the actual composer.

48: Under Schmitt, Hummel print: add date '1768 in Hummel's Thematic Cat.'. Add to Schmitt sources (4) Dunwalt Cat. 1770 (*cf.* 9) — 2 ob., 2 cor., str.

49: Add to Dittersdorf sources (2) *MS.* pts., St. Peter, Salzburg.

50: The Körzel parts are still extant (1761).

52: Under Haydn (1): A second *MS.* at Schwerin includes only the 4th, 5th and 6th movts. Add to Haydn sources (3) *MS.* pts., Donaueschingen.

53: *Modern edition:* Ed. by Adolf Sandberger, 'Münchner Haydn-Renaissance' Abt. I/2 (1937).

57: For 'Probable author' read *Correct author* and add (2) score of opera, Le Duc, Paris (pl. no. 83), 'Tragedie lyrique en trois actes Representée pour la première fois par l'Academie de Musique, le Mardi 25 Fevrier 1783' (copy *inter alia* in BM).

58: Under 'Probable author' add: *Franz Anton Rosetti* (1750–1792): Thematic Catalogue of 1804, Donaueschingen, Rosetti No. 10. *Modern editions* (as Haydn): (*a*) Ed. Adolf Sandberger, 'Münchner Haydn-Renaissance', Abt. I/4 (1939); (*b*) Ed. Hans Erdmann, Mitteldeutscher Verlag, Halle, 1955 (with an impossibly arrogant preface). *Tempo: Allegro* (*molto moderato*).

60: In the Bailleux print, this work is listed as No. II (not V). Lausenmayer (*recte*) was probably the double bass player in Richter's band at Strassbourg between 1769 and 1789. Add to Lausenmayer sources: *MS.* pts., Darmstadt.

61: *Tempo* is *Adagio maestoso*. The scoring is fl., 2 ob., 2 cor., 2 trpt., timp., str. vln. conc., 2 solo violas, vc. conc., str. *Probable author: Pichl* (*cf.* 1): (1) printed pts., Hummel, Amsterdam, 'Sinfonie Concertante . . . Œuvre VI' (pl. no. 523): copy in Washington, M.1001. P. 58, Op. 6–P; (2) *MS.* pts., Donaueschingen, Mus. ms. 1550.

62: Source (2) of Michael Haydn *MSS.* lacks the third movement.

67: In *incipit*, read for double dot in bar 1 a dotted quaver rest. *Correct author: Czibulka.* Either Alois Czibulka (1768–1845), the conductor in Ofen and Pest (now Budapest), or Matthaeus, born about 1770, studied in Prague, then Kapellmeister in Grätz (East Prussia) and, in 1798, Direktor of Buschen's Company (Gerber *Lexikon* 1812–1814 and Eitner). In the Donaueschingen Thematic Cat. of 1804, the Symphony is listed as 'Cibulka'; then the title-page of the actual parts seems to have disappeared, whereupon someone wrote Haydn's name in pencil on the vln. I part, and the work was promptly placed among the Haydn sources.

Later, the Cibulka entry in the Cat. was crossed out (since the work, as Cibulka, had disappeared). Thus, this D major Symphony never really existed as Haydn at all. *Literature:* H. Schorn, 'Neue Haydn-Funde' (*Neue Zeitschrift für Musik*, 1913, Nos. 34–35); Schorn did not see the Cibulka entry in the Donaueschingen Cat.

68: *Tempo* (in EH — see *infra*) *Allegro molto.* Under Haydn sources (2) read 'score' for 'parts'. *Probable author:* ? *Winkler:* MS. pts., EH (old Cat. No. 32/61) 'Sinfonia Ex D: Minor' (no fag.); *Franz Christian Neubauer* (1760–1795): MS. pts., Dresden (pts. anonymous, but Oels Cat. as Neubauer): see Hoboken.

71: The Haydn pts. at Donaueschingen are cat. Mus. ms. 737, 1 (not 708) and are entitled 'Di Sig: Haydn'; add (2) MS. pts., Madrid, Palacio Real, MS. 1973 (no Christian name).

74: Cancel the second source under Haydn (Frankfurt).

75: MS. pts. Donaueschingen, Mus. ms. 737, 2 as 'Del Sig Hayden'.

77: Add to Haydn sources (4) MS. pts., Prague Nat. Museum, cat. D223, 'Notturno' for str.

80: Source (1) includes three symphonies: Nos. (II) 90, 124 and 80.

81: *Tempo Largo sostenuto;* add *p*; last two notes of bar 2 should not be dotted; *tr* on *a flat*, bar 3. Scoring: str. only. *Probable author: Gaetano Pugnani* (1731– 1798): (1) printed pts., J. J. Hummel, Amsterdam and B. Hummel, Hague (no pl. no.) — 'Trè Quartetti à Due Violini, Alto Viola & Basso Continuo composte da G: Pugnani' (copy in BM, g. 687. a.(1).) (in Hummel's Thematic Cat. of 1768); (2) printed pts., same works, Welcker, London (copy in BM, RM 16.f.14.(3.)); (3) Dunwalt Cat., 1770 (*cf.* 9) as 'Quadro'; (4) printed pts., Venier, Paris, Op. 1, No. 2 (*N.B.* bar 2 is dotted here), 'Sei Sinfonie A 4. 5. e 7. Stromenti' (copy in Washington); for further sources, see Zschinsky-Troxler's standard work, *Gaetano Pugnani*, Berlin, 1939 (Atlantis Verlag).

83: Under Haydn: the pts. are anonymous and Haydn's name is nowhere to be seen, either on the cover, or on the parts. Jan LaRue has convincingly proved that this symphony is a work by *Baron Theodor von Schacht*; LaRue's definitive article on the subject was published in 1959 (*Music & Letters* Vol. 40, No. 2).

85: Add to Fränzl sources (2 Dunwalt Cat. 1770 (*cf.* 9), 2 fl., 2 cor., str. Add to Filtz sources: (3) Sigmaringen Cat. 1766, with 2 ob. and 2 cor.; (4) MS. pts., Rheda, cat. 918 (for Rheda, *cf.* 42).

89: Add to end of Haydn entry, 'later crossed out in Haydn's hand'. Add to Michael Haydn source (1), '4th movt. autograph, undated, also in EH'.

90: Add to Dittersdorf sources (4) Dunwalt Cat. 1770 (*cf.* 9), 2 fl., 2 cor., str.; (5) MS. pts., Florence Conservatorio, D 14/4; (6) MS. pts., Darmstadt; (7) MS. pts., Washington, M.1001, D.62.P. No. 5, marked 'Sig Ditters / Per la Capella Principale'.

94: Haydn, source (3), for 'pts.' read 'score'.

97: Add to Holzbauer sources (2) *MS.* pts., Rheda (*cf.* 42), *Allegro molto.*

99: This work is listed under Dittersdorf's name in the Sigmaringen Cat. 1766 (later addition).

100: Add to Pleyel sources (7) *MS.* pts., Washington, M.1001, P. 732P (Spanish Coll.).

101: For a discussion of this work and additional sources, see Landon, 'Two Orchestral Works' . . . MUSIC REVIEW, XVII/1 (1956).

104: Add to Pleyel sources (6) *MS.* pts., Darmstadt; (7) *MS.* pts., Washington, M.1001, P.731.P. (Spanish Coll.)

107: Under Jos. Haydn sources (4) should read: printed pts., Hummel ('Symph. Périodique No. XXIV' in a set of six by 'Diverses Auteurs') as *Mich.* Haydn; Br. Cat. 1772 lists the print as 'Hayden' with no Christian name; add to Jos. Haydn sources (9) Dunwalt Cat. 1770 (*cf.* 9), a later addition. The Mich. Haydn autograph was rediscovered by T. D. Thomas and is in the Bavarian State Library, Munich (Overture to *Die Hochzeit auf der Alm*); add to Mich. Haydn sources (4) authentic *MS.* pts. to the opera, St. Peter, Salzburg.

108: Add to Mich. Haydn sources (5) *MS.* score, Stockholm, and remove the words 'score &' from entry (3).

109: For the newly discovered Gyrowetz sources, see *supra*, pp. 29, 31.

110: under '*N.B.*' read '5' movts. (not 8).

111: Under Dittersdorf sources add (4) *MS.* pts., Regensburg.

112: Under Haydn sources add (2) *MS.* pts., Kroměříž (Kremsier), ČSR. Under Vaňhal sources, add (7) *MS.* pts., St. Peter, Salzburg; (8) printed pts., Hummel, 'Six Simphonies' — see I, 35, source 17 ('Sinfonia XXVII . . . S- Vanhal'); (9) *MS.* pts., Washington, M.1001, W.25P. (owner: 'Henkel') and *tempo Maestoso*; (10) *MS.* pts., Schlägl; (11) *MS.* pts., Donaueschingen mus. ms. 1990.

113: The signature on St. Peter parts should read 'Schripsit [*sic*] Bartholomaeus Ze inter [Zinter?] 1801'.

114: Add to Vaňhal sources (6) *MS.* pts., St. Peter, Salzburg; (7) *MS.* pts., Regensburg; (8) *MS.* pts., Donaueschingen, cat. Mus. ms. 328.

116: Add to Filtz sources (9) printed pts., Welcker, London, Nº 17 Gerrard St., St. Anns Soho (*c.* 1775), 'Six Simphonies' No. 1 (BM g. 474.m.(5.)); (10) Dunwalt Cat. 1770 (*cf.* 9); (11) Sarasin Cat., Basel; (12) *MS.* pts., Washington, M.1001, A2F. No. 11; (13) *MS.* pts., Donaueschingen, Mus. ms. 461 (2 clarinets, str.).

118: Add to Hofmann sources (4) Göttweig Cat., 1763, with no introduction (the *incipit* of the *Allegro molto*, A maj. 4/4, is not listed in my book). The scoring in Regensburg and Modena includes 2 ob. pts.

119: Add to Ordoñez sources (2) *MS.* pts., Donaueschingen, Mus. ms. 1482 ('In usum Franc. Car. Stuekle Rhetoris Candidati 1772'), str. only. See also p. 26, *supra.* The pts. probably from the former Benedictine Monastery of Villingen, secularized in 1803.

121: Cancel source (1) under Joseph Haydn sources, add (1) *MS.* pts., Donaueschingen ('Sig: Haydn') and (3) *MS.* pts., Zittau.

123: Under Mich. Haydn source (1) cancel the date. The first three movts. were finished on 27 September 1766 in Salzburg, and the Finale was added later, on 15 June 1772: (*incipit* follows) . . .

124: Under Haydn entry, cancel '*MS.*', add 'printed pts., Mme. Berault, Paris, Op. XIX: see *corrigendum* to II, 80, *supra.* Add to Dittersdorf sources (6) *MS.* pts., St. Peter, Salzburg; (7) Dunwalt Cat. 1770 (*cf.* 9), 2 fl., 2 cor., str.

131: Under Vaňhal sources, for (4) read: printed pts., 4 Sym., Op. XVI, Bureau d'Abbonement Musical, Paris, 1774 (this work is No. 4 of the set): announced in Br. Cat., *Announces* . . ., *Gazette* . . . in 1774.

132: Under Haydn sources add (2) *MS.* pts., dated 1766, Moravian Church Archives, Winston-Salem, North Carolina (a copy by J. F. Peter).

134: Under scoring, add '2 fag. in Pleyel sources'. Add to Pleyel sources (2) Sarasin Cat., Basel; (3) printed pts. 'Periodical Overture . . . as Perform'd at the Principal Concerts . . . Nᵒ [9]', London, Preston, 1794 (pl. no. 96): copy in BM h. 3210.(19.); (4) printed arr. for pf., vln. by F. Tomich., London, Longman & Broderip: copy in BM, g. 147.(11.); (5) printed arr. for pf., vln., fl. & vc. by S. F. Rimbault, London, W. Hodsoll (watermark date: 1823); (6) *MS.* pts., Harburg, dated 1789 together with (7) printed pts., Götz, Mannheim (pl. no. 185), Op. III No. 6; (8) *MS.* pts., Washington, M.1001, P.735.P (Spanish Coll.); (9) *MS.* pts., Donaueschingen, Mus. ms. 1586.

N.B.: I have not included any of the 'new' spurious symphonies found only in Hoboken, nor have I included half-a-dozen additional works which I have found, or readers have sent me; these are symphonies listed neither in my book nor in Hoboken's Catalogue. Similarly, this list of *errata* and *corrigenda* does not include new books and articles, especially since the Haydn Sesquicentenary will produce many important new additions to the (compared to that of the other masters) scanty Haydn literature which has appeared in the last fifty years.[1] The principal errors in the bibliography are as follows: *Beyle* and *Bombet* are both pseudonyms for *Stendhal*; for *Dale* read *Dab* and the date should be 1940 (XXI); *Gerber*, read *Lexikon* (not *Lexicon*); under *Hiller* read '*cf.* also "Periodicals" '; *Päsler*, date should read 1918; *Pohl, Denkschrift* — date should read 1871; *Ursin*, date should read 1929; *Zinzendorf*, for 'Vienna City Archives' read 'Staatsarchiv, Vienna'.

---

[1] The results have not yet (1960) been published, especially the important Congress papers of Bratislava and Budapest.

P. 861: Note to 18: I have just examined the score from Haydn's legacy, which is now in the Esterházy Archives, Budapest (temporary Cat. no. opera 714). Part of the score is obviously autograph, and there are many corrections and additions in Ordoñez' hand: this manuscript, incidentally, is the first bit of a musical autograph by Ordoñez that we have been able to locate. (After years' search, his autograph signature was discovered on a file in the Tonkünstler-Sozietät Archives, Vienna.) The EH source is entitled 'Musica / Della Parodia d'Alceste'. To my astonishment I found, in the first Act, the little *Balletto* entitled 'Menuetto in Tempo Com[m]odo e piano'[1] which also appears in Haydn's *Philemon und Baucis* (see *addendum,* p. 276, *supra*): In view of the fact that the other, rather similar piece has turned out to be by Gluck, I had assumed that the present *Menuetto* was also by Gluck. Obviously, it was composed by Carlos d'Ordoñez, that elusive and fascinating composer about whom I hope soon to write an article, with a complete thematic catalogue of his works — a project for which I have been collecting material for many years. The *incipit* of the piece in question is:

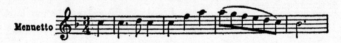

---

[1] The words 'e piano' are in Ordoñez' hand.

Sinfonia No. 33

Clarino I e II in C

From MSS. in Prague and Frankfurt-am-Main.
Joseph Haydn

II. Andante — Tacent

Sinfonia No. 33
Timpani in C-G
From MSS. in Prague and Frankfurt-am-Main.
Joseph Haydn

II. Andante — Tacet

Trio tacet. Menuetto da capo

Since this book is, in a way, an index to another book, it was not considered necessary to provide the present volume with an index of its own. Readers of *The Symphonies of Joseph Haydn* will be able to find any additional material in the present *Supplement* by using the original index together with the page references to the *addenda* and *corrigenda*.

As this book goes to press, we are able to make the announcement that all Haydn's symphonies are to be recorded on long-playing gramophone records. The project, conducted by Max Goberman and supervised by the author of this book, is to be issued by the American Library of Recorded Masterpieces on a subscription basis. The first series, containing Symphonies 6, 7, 8, 12, 13, 14, 40, 21, 22, 23, 24, 41, 51, 56, 60, 96 (original version) and 98 (original version), was recorded in Vienna with the State Opera Orchestra (which has been engaged for the entire series) in the Autumn of 1960. It is also planned to record, in another parallel series, all Haydn's operas, of which the first to be issued will be *L'infedeltà delusa*.